"a book for turning timid bystanders into ministers of mercy"

—John Dawson, from the Foreword

"For centuries, thoughtful people have been haunted by Jesus' story. Now Bob Maddux helps this haunting to be creative and productive. This book, like Jesus' story, will penetrate anyone who takes the time to sit under it."

—John Ortberg, author of *Everybody's Normal Till You Get to Know Them*

"From the treacherous roads of the Sixties Counterculture comes this insightful book offering medicine for a wounded world. In vivid writing, Bob Maddux bares his soul along with the soul of a generation and in so doing offers healing for every generation. Here in a frank look at our broken world, with dramatic stories culled from his own personal encounters, the author offers healing principles from the timeless parable of the Good Samaritan. Bob speaks from his years as a pastor and counselor but even more from the heart of one who's found his way home from his own perilous journey. Bob Maddux is my friend and when you finish reading this book, I believe you'll know why."

—Rich Wilkerson, Senior Pastor, Trinity Church, Miami Florida

"In this book Bob Maddux gives us a way to emotionally and spiritually connect with a world of hurting people. Beyond that, he shows how we can each help as he unpacks for us what he calls the "Good Samaritan's Kit." In it we find 'simple tools, but powerful medicine' to heal the wounded."

—Ken Blue, author of *Authority To Heal* and *Healing Spiritual Abuse*

"Here is a book that provides the adhesive by which shattered people can begin to find healing and wholeness. Writing from a rich background of personal encounters with the healing power of Christ, Pastor Maddux reflects the wisdom and insight of a seasoned and caring pastor. Follow the life-giving stories of this book, and your life will be challenged and inspired with hope and peace."

—Richard Dresselhaus, Executive Presbyter, Assemblies of God

"Bob Maddux takes us on a whole new ride down an old highway through his imaginative contemporary and biographic sketches of the classic Scripture story. Millennia later, thieves that strike, strip, and leave us for dead have not gone away. Revisiting this dangerous road we all still must travel, Good Samaritan Therapy points us clearly and squarely back to the One with the only real qualification to love us, heal us, and set us out strong once more on the souls' journey Home."

—Winkie Pratney, author of *Youth Aflame! Handbook for Followers of Jesus*

GOOD SAMARITAN THERAPY

REAL MEDICINE FOR THE SOUL

BOB MADDUX

LEAFWOOD
PUBLISHERS

GOOD SAMARITAN THERAPY
Real Medicine for the Soul

Copyright © 2004 by Bob Maddux

ISBN 0-9728425-9-4
Printed in the United States of America

Cover design by Mark Decker, Moe Studio, Siloam Springs, AR

For information:
Leafwood Publishers
1409 Hunter Ridge
Siloam Springs, AR 72761
1-877-634-6004 (toll free)

Visit our website: www.leafwoodpublishers.com

04   05   06   07   08   09   7   6   5   4   3   2   1

Dedication

To Claudia for all the oil and wine over the last 34 years. To Jonathan, Rachel and Jessica for staying with us on the journey. To the congregation at CLA for believing in our vision. And to Stan and Shirley for sharing their advice, support and pancakes.

FOREWORD

by John Dawson

Bob and his wife Claudia have nurtured people to emotional and spiritual health for over 30 years. They are gentle, joyous people who have provided safe haven for many wounded souls. I have seen them restore fallen leaders, adopt the lonely and guide people through tragedy and loss. As local church pastors they have seen the restoration of broken lives occur daily.

I recommend this book for two reasons. First, because it is delightfully warmhearted and easy to read. Second, because it contains proven answers. This is not a complex, theoretical tome; it's more like a wise letter from a loving father.

Using the parable of the Good Samaritan recorded in Luke 10, Bob answers the question, "How do I heal the wounded traveler? Where do I find the tools to put a life back together?"

You may be a traveler needing help or a healer seeking a handbook that will guide you in helping others. This book serves both needs. Fascinating stories are combined with understandable steps toward restoration, practical steps illustrated by helpful, sometimes dramatic, anecdotes from contemporary culture. This is a good read that informs and inspires along the way.

Are you willing to risk loving again? Is it worth renewing the quest for wholeness? Is there hope? Bob points out that religious places aren't always safe; just as "the Jericho Road was fraught with dangers, so are churches. Such places can be risky to one's emotional well being if they are merely religious. Frequently, they're filled with wounded people seeking refuge and wounded people can wound others," he writes.

Perhaps the greatest value of this book is that it challenges wounded people to rise above their pain, to take a risk for the sake of love. It calls us to look beyond the dangers and see our role in healing others.

In churches there is an unmobilized army of people who long to help others yet draw back in fear. Anticipating failure and not knowing where to begin, we remain impotent. This is a book for turning timid bystanders into ministers of mercy.

Outside the church, legions of people who feel degraded by the snares of modern culture are unaware of the transforming power of God. Thinking they know the limits of "shallow religious tradition," they have dismissed the possibility that God is personal, knowable and deeply committed to the transformation of any person who turns to Him.

It is my prayer that many wounded travelers will be given this book in their darkest hour and then discover for the first time who animated the hearts of the Good Samaritans of yesterday and today.

As a missionary I have observed the healing power of God working in the lives of the followers of Jesus in slums, refugee camps and war zones. In those desperate places, the reality of Christ's resurrection and present ministry seems starkly obvious. My compassion goes out, however, to the people far from such places. It's the affluent life that seduces the heart into spiritual dullness and unbelief.

Devastating wounds can be covered with the gloss of popular modernity. Take for example the practice of "dating." Many people pass into their twenties having experienced something parallel to multiple divorces.

This book may trigger painful memories. But maybe it's time the forgotten foundations of your life were cleansed and healed. Read on. You are in good hands.

John Dawson, President
Youth With A Mission, International

CONTENTS

INTRODUCTION

Emerging from antiquity is a unique story of suffering and recovery. It goes something like this . . .

His first flicker of consciousness is stabbing pain. It comes from everywhere. His ribs ache. His back and arms shriek for relief. His head pounds like bellows made of steel. Stones press into his backside like blunt spears. Blood slowly flows from cuts and lacerations left by the bandits' weapons. Then there's humiliation. He's been robbed and left naked in the road. He feels helpless and alone. He can sense his life force going quickly. Nearby, the death angel seems to whisper his name. Perhaps the end will come shortly. Then the grip of blackness pulls him back into unconsciousness. But even in this false rest

13

there is toil. Dreams become nightmares and from them emerge fantasies of relief. Such mercy is soon over. He's awake again and this time there is no escape from the pain. Tears come from the core of his soul but his voice can only whimper.

Through the murkiness of his struggle a shadowy figure passes by near him. It's gone before he can find the strength to cry out. Then another. This time a face hovers over him. Its expression looks perplexed, almost sympathetic. But it's soon gone as well. Now he feels truly alone. Alone like he's never felt before. Somewhere, some strange and sinister gong seems to be ringing out the last moments of his life. Blackness. Pain. Death.

Then unexpectedly he senses the presence of someone else. There's love in the touch. A voice reassures him. He can feel soothing ointment and searing pain as oil and wine mix. Slowly but firmly cloth is bound into place closing his wounds. Then he is being lifted and set on an animal and gently led up the path. Fits of awareness come and go. An inn appears before his eyes. A bed. More oil, more bandages and always the kind words.

Days later he finds he's healing, surrounded by the care of an innkeeper, his rescuer nowhere in sight. What an odd end to a treacherous journey.

*　　*　　*　　*　　*

Life is risky and its roads dangerous. The lonely traveler described above discovered this the hard way. Most of us do. We've all had our run-ins with "robbers" of one kind or another. Many of us limp home and try to find healing. Many of us are still limping, our scars hidden. They're buried deep and it hurts when we talk about them. We'd rather forget about the treachery we found on the lonely road.

Jesus talked about this road. The story is found in the Gospel of Saint Luke.

> 30 *In reply Jesus said: "A man was going down from Jerusalem to Jericho, when he fell into the hands of robbers. They stripped him of his clothes, beat him and went away, leaving him half dead.* 31 *A priest happened to be going down the same road, and when he saw the man, he passed by on the other side.* 32 *So too, a Levite, when he came to the place and saw him, passed by on the other side.* 33 *But a Samaritan, as he traveled, came where the man was; and when he saw him, he took pity on him.* 34 *He went to him and bandaged his wounds, pouring on oil and*

15

*wine. Then he put the man on his own donkey,
took him to an inn and took care of him.* [35] *The
next day he took out two silver coins and gave
them to the innkeeper. 'Look after him,' he said,
'and when I return, I will reimburse you for any
extra expense you may have.'"*

(Luke 10:30-35, NIV)

How do you heal the wounded traveler? Where do
you find the tools to put a soul back together? Two men
on that road didn't know where to begin. The priest and
the Levite seemed to lack both the concern and the time.
But perhaps they also lacked the skill. At times I've found
myself lacking all three things. But, like many, once Jesus
came, all that began to change. I began to find the heart
and the time but still lacked the skill. For those of us who
need such skill, God's word provides it.

There's a secret in this parable of Jesus. Like all his stories it can be taken on different levels. At first glance it
offers a piercing commentary on prejudice, the nature of
true friendship and social responsibility. But as I've medi-
tated on this story over the years, I've discovered much
more. Over my 30 years in full-time ministry I've found in
its simple narrative some tools of healing and a prescription for the mending of wounded souls. In the Samaritan's

16

first-century "first aid" kit lies medicine for the psyche.

What could the Good Samaritan do for his patient on the lonely hillside of Judea? Five simple things:

- bind up his wounds
- pour in oil
- pour in wine
- take him to an inn and care for him there
- leave behind resources for his ongoing needs

It sounds simplistic doesn't it? Yet it worked and Jesus recommended it. Can such therapy have a parallel in the realm of the soul? I think it does. There are principles here that can bring us healing. I was once a lonely, wounded traveler. My healing has taken time. For good reason, the wounds were deep. But I've found medicine in this parable. It's something that worked not only for me but others who've sought to recover from the "bloody way."

This book has a simple goal: To equip you with tools of healing and, in so doing, to make you a Good Samaritan. You'll not only be able to help others, but perhaps you'll find healing for yourself as well. Although it won't give you a degree in psychology or the prestige of a licensed counselor, it can provide some real medicine prescribed by the Great Physician.

ONE

THE ROAD

"A man was going down from Jerusalem to Jericho . . ."

Well, Georgia Sam he had a bloody nose
Welfare Department they wouldn't give him no clothes
He asked poor Howard where can I go
Howard said there's only one place I know
Sam said tell me quick man I got to run
Ol' Howard just pointed with his gun
And said that way down on Highway 61.

"Highway 61 Revisited"
Bob Dylan

The road was notorious. It was nicknamed the "bloody way." It linked Jerusalem and the priestly suburb of Jericho. Strange that such a highway would be dangerous, yet terror had found a home on its twisting steps. Travelers on it were fearful. One such traveler found his fears coming true. Jesus in the Gospel of Saint Luke describes it tersely but graphically. In a burst of force his assailants were upon him. The thieves swiftly finished their work and then abandoned him. Wounded, naked and half dead he lay there as strangers passed by—first a priest and then a Levite. He found little sympathy from either. Finally, a Samaritan, one considered a social outcast, stopped and from his meager supplies began the process of restoring life to the wounded man.

I'd read the parable many times. But one time its tragic story took on a whole new significance for me. I began to picture a similar road. One I'd been on. One where I'd been wounded and left for dead. The wounds were painful and the thieves, though they were not as obvious to the eye, left me stripped and naked. In the late 1960's I had explored a deeply pagan lifestyle and found myself with profound emotional and psychological injuries. In the years since, I've met many people who trekked those same roads, whole generations scattered along the highways of our culture. Often they have experienced little more compassion than the lonely traveler in Jesus' story. They have heard from a throng of counselors and psychologists. They have offered a host of solutions. But many of us still bleed and die while our therapists seem little more than religious strangers staring down at our pain.

When I first became a Christian I joined a small church on the wrong side of the tracks. It was filled with delightful people, most of whom had come from rural backgrounds. I found myself drawn towards one Mexican-American family. Their open hearts and happy children were like a magnet to anyone looking for friendship. They were the kind of people who take in strangers.

But one time this kind-heartedness put the father of this family in great peril. Driving along a California highway, he saw a group of men signaling for help. They had apparently broken down and were in need of assistance.

To reach out to others with acts of mercy, we must overcome obstacles like fear, prejudice and apathy.

Being a compassionate man and lacking what some would call wisdom, he pulled over to help them. He soon discovered that they wanted more than assistance. He was assaulted, robbed and left severely wounded. His recovery was difficult.

The memory of this man and his lovely family stick with me to this day. I still wonder why anyone would want to harm such a loving man. His tragic encounter left many questions in my own mind and a deepening sense of wariness about human nature.

As you read this parable of Jesus you probably noticed that it deals with people who were very religious. Religion is supposed to offer help for the afflicted. Frequently it does. And when it does it should go by its more biblical name: True Religion. The book of James says that true religion cares for widows and orphans and is not spotted by corruption (James 1:27). But it's very easy to be merely religious. This seems to be the trouble with some of the inhabitants of Jericho. Historical records claim that it was home to 12,000 priests. For some of its inhabitants their religion was formal and lacked the power of true compassion. The priest and Levite no doubt lived there. You would think that a road linking two such religious cities would be safer. But religious places are not necessarily safe. My visit to the city of Jerusalem confirmed that. Here where Bible history meets the face of modern politics, I found a sense of fear and foreboding. One of the most religious places in the world was also one of the most dangerous.

There was good reason to feel fear on the "bloody way." The Priests and Levites, of course, could have been targets themselves. Their own anxiety could have kept them from stopping to help. This is the issue we all face. At what point do we allow compassion to move us beyond our fears? Reaching out to others with acts of mercy is at the heart of this story. To do this, though, we must overcome obstacles like fear, prejudice and apathy. If we don't, and still claim to be a follower of God, we will be practicing mere religion, not true religion.

Religious places aren't always safe. Just as the Jericho road was fraught with dangers, so are churches. Such places can be risky to one's emotional well being if they are merely religious. Frequently they are filled with wounded people seeking refuge, and wounded people can wound others.

This wonderful parable challenges us to take risks. It calls us to look beyond the dangers and see our role in healing. You may want to help others, yet your fears hold you back. You may not know where to begin. You wonder: "What will happen to me if I try to help someone?" "Will I be hurt in the process?" "I've been hurt before and I don't want to be hurt again." Such questions might keep most of us from attempting such "risky" love.

Let me suggest a first step by taking a closer look at Jesus' story. He described what the lonely traveler on the Jericho road went through. He outlined in vivid detail its violent process. Perhaps by exploring it and its consequences we'll not only find a greater compassion for those who have been hurt but also gain some insight on how to bring healing to them.

In the next five chapters we'll take a closer look at the mugging. Although this investigation may seem gruesome at times, it's part of the procedure that will lead us to real answers. There's good news ahead but first the bad news.

TWO

THIEVES

"A man was going down from Jerusalem to Jericho,
when he fell into the hands of robbers . . ."

That woman you've been loving, she was another man's
You stole her heart while his back was turned
On every corner there's an outlaw waiting
Who wants to teach you what you never learned

"No Honor Among Thieves"
Toby Keith

Thieves. Literature and film have often glorified them. But for anyone who's even come close to being mugged, there's little glory in it. I've never been the victim of violent robbers. But in the late sixties I had an experience that gave me a strong taste of the terror and loss that befell the man on the Jericho road.

It was a clear and breezy day as I stood along Highway 1 on the California coast south of San Francisco. The sky was blue and the fresh salt air intoxicating. To my drug-influenced worldview it was the perfect day in a fantasy world that seemed to have no end. I was hitchhiking my way back from a weekend of music and partying at a friend's house in Santa Cruz. In those days I weighed all of 129 pounds and on my 5' 10" 1/2" frame that weight barely held my bones together. I looked as fragile on the outside as I felt on the inside at that moment. In spite of my fantasy I wasn't finding a ride. So I continued to stand there, a scarecrow in hippie garb, one thumb bravely held out to the flow of traffic. A few record albums and a bamboo flute were stuffed under my arms. To pass the time I improvised on my flimsy instrument, mixing my own melodies with the sound of the surf and seagulls.

Waiting for a ride on the side of the road is a lonely and intimidating process. Most people seem to pass and stare as if you were another piece of the scenery. After awhile you wonder if anyone will stop and, if so, what kind of person will it be. Eventually an older model car pulled off the road. It was filled with teenagers a few years younger than myself. No sooner had I gotten in the car than I discovered that it was more than age that separated us. They appeared to be a group of coastal rednecks looking for mischief. They were noticeably drunk and belligerent, and showed clear disdain for my hippie attire and hair. We hadn't gone further than a few miles when they turned off the main road and headed into a sparsely populated woodland stretching away from the coast. They made some lame excuse about needing to run an errand. But it was obvious to me that something was amiss.

The tension in the car increased and so I put my flute to my quivering lips. Perhaps I could calm the savage beasts. Their laughter soon punched a whole in that day dream. Then it happened, what I'd been dreading. They missed their turn off, one that probably led to an even more isolated spot. Their leader, riding shotgun in the front seat, soon exploded in anger and demanded that they pull over. He began screaming at me. Emerging from the front seat, he jerked open my door and pulled me from the car. He grabbed my record albums. One quick blow and they were in pieces. Next he shattered my flute across his knee. Then he started in on me. He kicked and struck me several times. I wasn't much of a fighter in those days. But I was wiry and hard to hold on to. If he hadn't been drunk and if his buddies had moved more quickly, I would no doubt have ended up like my flute and albums.

Terror is an amazing thing. It produces adrenalin by the buckets full. Mine were running over. Outnumbered and left with little to defend myself, I did what any brave but skinny hippie would do. I ran screaming towards the closest house. It was up a hill through a thicket of underbrush and weeds. My tormentors struggled to follow me and soon lost heart. Once they saw that I had escaped they jumped into their car and sped away. The shocked homeowner, accompanied by his bewildered children, spilled out of the house and came to my aid. They allowed me to phone my friend who picked me up a short time later and saw that I got home safely.

I can still remember my numbed state of mind that day. I have a better understanding of the terror of being robbed and brutalized. My attackers didn't steal much from me that day. All I really lost were my albums and a cheap flute. But I was stunned. Stunned that my fantasy world could be so quickly shattered. Stunned that the halcyon days of the late sixties could be a dangerous place. Stunned that I was a target of hate and misunderstanding.

Other than a few bruises, all that remained with me was a strong sense of paranoia towards the "straight world." My physical wounds faded but the emotional ones grew deeper. I had lost something that day. It had been stolen in a few moments of terror near Highway 1. But looking back now it's nothing compared to what other events in my life have stolen. In fact I've discovered that I live in a world of people who've fallen among thieves. In the process of life they have been stripped of a host of things that could have made them healthy.

It often starts when they are young, in their first years at school, and continues the rest of their lives. Friends leave and take precious things with them. Social bullies control and manipulate them. Parents abuse and guilt-trip them. Leaders and teachers disappoint them. The world in general can be unjust and cold. All this can rob us of hope, trust and love. If you're like most people, such thieves are not new to you. You've had your share of run-ins with them. But, perhaps like a lot of people, you still haven't found a way of restoring what you've lost to them.

I never went back to pick up my shattered musical treasures. If I had, perhaps I could have learned something from those broken remains. My tormentors had a goal in mind, however conscious or unconscious they were of it. They wanted to steal more than my possessions. They wanted to steal my soul. When the thieves on the Jericho road fell upon the lonely traveler, that was only the beginning of his sorrows. They soon took the next step in their plan.

THREE

STRIPPING

"They stripped him of his clothes . . ."

Are we just running from the pain
Or do we see just what we are
We're naked in the rain
Naked in the rain

"Naked in the Rain"
Ronnie James Dio

Thieves are covetous. They take what others have. I think of Sally (not her real name). From all outward appearances she seems the perfect picture of a wholesome and attractive young woman. Her smile is sweet and her demeanor gentle. But as she sits and shares her story with me, I realize that she's been robbed. Robbed years before in her childhood, and what was stolen is still missing. Sally was the victim of an abusive father and a series of step-fathers. More than innocence was stripped as they took away her "clothes" all those years ago. Her dignity, her virginity and her self-worth went with it. Since then she has tried to find worth in a series of relationships and wild living. None of them has satisfied. She's a Christian now and we'd be tempted to say that her problems are over. But that would be far from the truth. She still must pick up the pieces of her shattered soul and through God's grace rebuild her world.

I've seen many like her. Often in the euphoria of the early days of their Christian life, the pain of the past is masked under the newness of the church's care. But there are still things that must be dealt with. There are monsters in the closet that will emerge and must be faced. What's been stolen must be restored and what's been broken must be mended.

Satan was a thief from the beginning. First he tried to steal God's glory. Then, hurled from heaven, he sought to steal the glory with which God had clothed man. He succeeded and ever since has been attempting to steal what little humanity man has left. Every now and then we read or hear some great story of human kindness and courage. But just as often we come across the tragic tales of people who do unspeakable things to others. Accounts of mothers who have drowned their infants in a lake or bathtub. Stories of fathers who beat their babies to death in a fit of rage or teenagers who abuse each other or their elderly parents.

Then there are lesser deeds of evil, deeds that take place every day in our ordinary world. Vicious words that bruise. Hardened hearts that refuse to give affection to a spouse, a child, a friend. Indifference to the suffering of others. Selfish attitudes that push others in the pursuit of personal glory.

There's no excuse for such behavior, but one must still ask where these monsters come from and what produces their ugly deeds. I believe they come from people who've been robbed. Something, somewhere has been stripped from their psyche.

At a youth missions training center I came across a young man who bared his soul to me in a letter. I'd spoken on the power of imagination and the dangerous things that can happen when it's not expressed under the creative genius of God.

His two-page note told the story of his slide into decadence. It started when he and his friends became fascinated with the cheap "B" type movies of blood and horror.

Soon those weren't thrilling enough. And slowly, but unrelentingly, his humanity began to be stripped away. Next they delved into snuff films—watching in fascination as someone was murdered. How do you find pleasure in such things unless you've been robbed? At what point was he stripped of that very human garment that God clothes each one of us with when we enter this world?

The young man was a committed Christian now, but I could tell that this experience had robbed him and that, years later, he was still seeking in some way to pull the fabric of his soul back into place.

Then there was a news story I read about the discovery of a truckload of human embryos on their way across a national border. Investigators found that this load of human death was headed to a factory where they were to be turned into shampoo, hair care and other cosmetic products. Confronted by these sorts of tragedy we start to realize that we've all been robbed. Something has stolen our love for human life. It's us, our culture…our family life…our mothers who have, tragically, been stripped of a natural affection for unborn babies.

But it's not just the startling examples that draw my attention to our dilemma but the common ones as well. The parents who quietly shut out their children while pursuing career and status. Friends who betray their buddies because they've become unsuccessful.. A culture that increasingly equates happiness with lots of sex, money or physical attractiveness. TV programs that revel in humiliating people. Shows that create large audiences that seem to delight in emotional gangbanging. All these can work their way into our souls and rip us off. But as horrible as it is to strip someone of their clothing, there are greater crimes. Crimes from which many people never recover. Such robbery is all too often only the beginning of crimes against our souls.

FOUR

WOUNDING

"They stripped him of his clothes, beat him. . . "

You have left a blazing trail
If you had been a hammer
I'd be a broken nail
You gave me nothing—
Nothing but regrets
Don't think it's over—
It's not over yet

> "You Hurt Me & I Hate You"
> The Eurythmics

For I am poor and needy,
and my heart is wounded within me.

> Ps 109:22, NIV

A man's spirit sustains him in sickness,
but a crushed spirit who can bear?

> Prov. 18:14, NIV

Warriors on the field of battle wound their opponents for a clear reason. They wound to conquer. Their weapons are fashioned with obvious intent. Hardened. Sharpened. Targeted. Anyone who's ever been wounded knows how accurate they can be and how deeply they can hurt.

Wounds on the battlefield of love have a similar effect. One such wound left a young man in a Sacramento area high school its tragic victim. My family and I had just moved to this central California city when I came across his heartrending story in a local newspaper. Grief stricken over his lover's jilting, he waited at her home with a loaded gun. As she emerged from her house he emptied the revolver's deadly missiles into her body. Then he sat on the curb and waited for the police. When they asked him why he had murdered his girlfriend he simply stated, "All she wanted me for was sex." Now that she had dumped him, it seems he couldn't stand the thought of her with someone else.

There is no justification for this angry young man's actions, but there is plenty of evidence for his motives. Sex with someone does one of two things. It either deeply bonds us with them or creates a kind of callousness that makes us unable to bond. Such insensitive people jump from relationship to relationship, caring little for those they wound and appearing to rarely if ever become truly intimate with someone. But this young man had obviously bonded with his paramour, and the breakup had left him broken.

Most craftsmen know the principle of bonding. Modern glues, when used to bind two pieces of wood together, create such a strong joint that any attempt to sever them by force usually leaves a break in one. Things never seem to split at the place of union. So it was with the broken young man whose soul was wounded and all he could understand was the pain and whose only solution seemed to be violence. His obvious inability to control his sexual passion was soon matched by his similar inability to control his rage. His wound was so deep and painful that any sense of concern for his former partner's well being was gone. It had been a selfish love, followed by an even greater form of selfishness: revenge. His moral center had been knocked unconscious.

We may not use guns, but many wound each other every day. In a culture obsessed with pleasure we become easy targets for such warfare. The writer of Proverbs left advice for those who would be entangled by such deadly devices. He warned his young offspring to avoid sexual sin: "Whoever commits adultery with a woman lacks understanding; he who does so destroys his own soul" (Prov. 6:32, NKJV).

Sexual sin exposes us to arrows that pierce deeply and often cannot be removed. They destroy the soul. Put simply they perforate the fabric of one's personhood—one's mind, emotions, and will. The things that make you uniquely you are marred. There were two victims in our Sacramento story. The girl, although not innocent of all sin, found herself the target of a bitter temper; her jilted lover found himself the victim of a wounded soul. His injury had been self-inflicted and unjustified but nonetheless deadly.

> *"Whoever commits adultery with a woman lacks understanding; he who does so destroys his own soul." Prov. 6:32*

Could he not have dealt with it in another way? Of course. Thousands do every day. But his rage is a picture of what so many face all the time. We give ourselves and then we're betrayed. And finding ourselves thus wounded we have few apparent options. We run away in some other indulgence, we hate those we formerly worshiped or we grow a callous to cover the scars. Perhaps it is just such experiences that Peter was attempting to warn his readers about in his first letter: "Dear friends, I urge you, as aliens and strangers in the world, to abstain from sinful desires, which war against your soul" (1 Peter 2:11, NIV).

There is warfare against the soul. Your sensibilities can be scarred. The world of relationships can be a battlefield that leaves you exposed to incoming fire that will shred your innermost parts.

I personally can remember experiencing some of this in my youth. I was fresh out of high school and hormonally saturated like most guys my age. Sexual mores had changed drastically in the mid 60's and I, for one, was glad. The fantasies of my teen years began to be realized in the form of several willing girls. One left a deep impression on my life. Let's call her Misty (not her real name). She was the classic picture of a teenage boy's fantasy. A prom princess, who bore a certain gushing femininity modeled after the sex kittens of the silver screen. Previously I had only dreamed that such girls could be mine to ravish. But the promiscuous atmosphere of 1964 and my new identity as a social maverick gave me a mystique that had attracted her.

We both abandoned other lovers and consummated our relationship on our first encounter. The experience had all the elements of a romantic and passionate fairytale. A moonlit night. The balmy atmosphere of summer evening's air after a hot valley day. A convertible and lots of hormones. It all seemed like a dream to me. She was there for the taking. But I was the one being taken. We fell deeply in lust. And although we both had other relationships during our affair, me especially, one thing was certain. I had bonded with Misty. I can still remember long, lonely treks, hitch hiking home on highway 99 to see her on the weekends between classes. I loved this girl.

But one day she tired of me and broke off our relationship. Half my soul went with her. I was in pain deeper than I'd ever experienced. I wasn't about to kill her, but the arrows had gone deep and I was a mess. Sure, life went on. Other lovers came. But there would be an open wound there for some time. Like the lonely traveler on the road to Jericho, I had allowed myself, through my own foolishness, to be brutalized by the bandits that take your most valuable possession: your soul.

The next few years of the 60's were a whirlwind of experimentation with drugs and alternative lifestyles. All of these were only a temporary salve for my hurts. Not until I encountered the "lover of my soul" did I find someone who would heal my wounds. Such healing is the lesson at the heart of this book.

Other bandits lurk on the roads of existence. Drugs wound just as surely and deeply. Alcohol abuse has left its victims in every generation, but the psychedelics of the 60's left a level of spiritual exploitation previously unknown. Mental health wards are full of those who never returned from the grand adventure of the "flower" generation. These experiments were just as hurtful as the emotional pain of broken relationships. They produce a kind of lost-ness that leaves the traveler stranded forever. Not only is one wounded and left for dead, there's no map for the way home.

I still remember the account in a major news magazine about the hopeless druggie who, after taking one too many acid trips, thought he was an orange. He was convinced that if anyone squeezed him he would turn into orange juice. It sounds hilarious if it weren't true. But if you've seen some of the sad souls I've dealt with as a halfway house director in my early years in ministry, you'd feel different. Working with the victims of the counterculture, I saw that such fantasies are fierce realities. I had to bring people down from flights of terror.

43

Reviewing again the bandit's tactics, the plan is clear. Attack suddenly, wound deeply and leave your victim half dead. Let the elements finish him off.

To illustrate this point allow me to visit again a very personal part of my history. Like a lot of youth in my generation, I quickly succumbed to the allure of illicit drugs. Maverick psychologists like Timothy Leary and an emerging pop culture not only gave legitimacy to their use but also created a positive spin for such experimentation. Cheap enlightenment. Lots of ecstasy. "Help build a better world through chemistry." The motto of a rebel generation that lacked any real hardship and the type of wisdom it produces. We were soon to learn that such experimentation never let us off easy. We've all heard the horror stories about the catatonic in some metal ward who never came back from his last trip to psychedelic never-never land. But for many of us who did make it back, we found our minds and emotions less than whole.

My own odyssey began with marijuana and went on to the mother of all psychedelics, LSD. The trips were great at first. Full of new insight—most of which was gone once the drug wore off. Every now and then one ended dull and somber. But there were demons out there. Real and imagined. And each time I faced them it seemed a little more of

44

my trust and hope were eaten away. I've heard of children who've been traumatized by war and find the sound of gunfire an immediate trigger of serious stress. People in such situations lose their anchor. I lost mine one day.

It was one of those idyllic afternoons in San Francisco. I wandered through Golden Gate park with a friend. Ponds in the Oriental gardens took on a beauty and symmetry that was otherworldly and soon downright frightening. But they also seemed to promise liquid bliss. The echoes and haunting voices from the ether world seemed to come closer. But I pushed them aside as I had in the past. Later in what I'd hoped would be an ultimate jam session, our electric guitars became sinister. I set mine down as if it had become a slithering reptile. Glancing in a mirror I saw my face contort and melt. I'd had such visions before but this time something inside snapped. My courage dissolved. The seas of bliss now turned into lakes of fire and I was all alone. Even my friend's attempts at help proved futile, even frightening. One minute he had been a buddy, the next a vessel of demonic torment.

I fled the house and soon fled all attempts at psychedelic enlightenment. But I didn't leave without wounds. My basic trust had fled as well. The sort of innocence that God puts in children and grows balanced in healthy adults

45

had vanished. Time would restore some of it, but only the Good Samaritan offered a permanent solution. Such healing balm is another story at the heart of this book.

I was not alone on the "hippy trail" of the 60's. Many of my fellow travelers have gone on to become everything from stock brokers to school teachers. But we bear the scars of our travels. And much of what our progeny have inherited from such selfish lifestyles does not bode well for the corporate psyche. Broken marriages, unrelenting hedonism, and jingoistic pursuit of greed all are signs of the wounds we received on the lonely roads of the 60's and 70's. We're still not healthy and it shows. We replaced our drugs and sex with safer pursuits but carry our wounds with us.

What about all the other wounded travelers who now join us on the roads of the new millennium? The promiscuous trails that my generation scouted in the 60's have become superhighways. The victims are just as frequent. One thing is a little different. Wounded people in this era can find lots of apparent compassion. Counselors and new age therapies are everywhere. But are we any less injured and any healthier? It's doubtful. We've glossed over the scars and found new cosmetics to cover the torn tissue of emotion. But as a pastor I see bleeding everywhere. We need healing. Jesus' prescription in Luke offers true medicine. Having been healed by it I can honestly say, "God's cure is the best one out there." But one has to follow the doctor's orders for the cure to work.

The bandits on the Jericho road no doubt beat their victim about the head and body. But there's a deeper trauma. Many of us have been beaten mentally and emotionally by soulish marauders. Such beatings can begin even before we have the ability to realize we're victims.

I've shared some graphic stories of those who've seemed to push life over the edge. But I've also seen much brokenness and hurt in those who grow up in "safe" places. They haven't taken drugs or experimented with alternative lifestyles, but they've still become victims, fellow travelers on the "Jericho road."

> *"The words of a talebearer are as wounds, and they go down into the innermost parts of the belly."* Prov. 18:8

When I first began pastoring in Southern California, I came across one deeply wounded life. Outwardly she appeared normal. She loved animals and her gentle spirit seemed to speak of a quiet but vital faith. Soon, though,

I found myself counseling with her and her husband. What I discovered under that placid outer shell was shocking. Her self worth was gone and her many tears shouted at me of an abuse that had started in her childhood. Her father had been a brutal man. He had not physically struck her but his words had been like fists pounding on a gentle heart. No affirmation, only condemnation. He always told her how worthless she was, that she would never amount to anything. The very one designated by God to love and nurture her had regularly betrayed that responsibility.

Such betrayals leave us so fearful that we soon build walls around that tender spot. We vow that we won't be hurt again. We will never let anyone close enough to us to hurt us. No one will know our secrets. No one will know us at all. As an adult this legacy had left her ill equipped to deal with the normal challenges of marriage. The grief of her youth was eating into the heart of her home.

In one way or another we've all known similar betrayal. It may not have been as brutal but it has left us suspicious. We've been wounded by what the King James Bible calls a talebearer. To put it in modern terms, a back stabbing, two-faced, tongue-wagging gossip. Proverbs well describes these actions: "The words of a talebearer are as wounds, and they go down into the innermost parts of the belly" (Prov. 18:8, KJV).*

Strong's Hebrew dictionary defines the original Hebrew word for "wounds" as "to burn in or to rankle." So it appears that the words of a talebearer can scorch like an inner fire. What do talebearers do? They usually carry some tidbit of scandalous information, the latest gossip. The current update on who's failed or sinned. Or just juicy bites of character-damaging facts. But it's what such information does to us when we hear it second hand that explains its dangerous quality. *Words carry power.*

We've all been in a group of people we've considered our friends and experienced something like what I'm about to describe. The conversation is pleasant, playful and reassuring. But when one of the group excuses himself we unexpectedly find the conversation changing. Perhaps it's just an idle comment about some idiosyncrasy of the person who's just left the group. But it's soon followed by other critical statements about the person's character or looks. These tales have a double edge to them. If they ever get back to the accused person, it's easy to picture the wounds such statements would cause.

But what is also so caustic about this kind of conversation is the atmosphere it creates among those who hear it. Who would ever want to share their real thoughts with such "friends"? "I can't really let them know what I think. What do they say about me when I'm not here?" We've been rankled. Our hearts burn with the fire of shame. Of course we all need to have tougher skin while keeping our hearts tender. But all too often such social environments have an opposite effect. We build walls and safeguards around us to last a lifetime. In our attempt to protect ourselves, we shut ourselves up in a sterile and lonely world. We end up stunted and fearful and the world loses someone who could bring it another song of joy.

Calluses can also grow on our heart when we choose to indiscriminately expose ourselves to brutal and caustic images. Video game junkies can sometimes develop a core of insensitivity. Watch enough slasher movies and you can develop the social conscience of an Orc. Of course, I'm overstating the point. But why do I see such lack of compassion and apathy in this generation that has grown up with the flash and pop of special effects and a constant flow of gruesome images? Even if the connection is slight, it still leaves me concerned for the souls of a generation feeding on a diet of horror films and brutal computer games.

Other things come to wound us as well. We can be struck just as deeply by situations not of our own making.

Life is full of hurtful things that none of us ever go searching for. Existence seems to wound us indiscriminately. We grow up in a neighborhood full of bullies. We didn't choose to be raised there. Our parents chose it for us. We suffer the consequences. We find employment at a firm that promises a healthy work environment. Later we discover our boss is a control freak or some of our fellow employees have their own agenda. They intimidate us to assure their own advancement. They lie about us behind our back for the simple pleasure of seeing us suffer. We discover enemies in the hallways of our schools and angry people in the pews of our churches. Life's roadways are hazardous. Hurtful situations greet us with a punch to our emotional solar plexus.

Several years ago I was invited to speak at a dynamic church on the East Coast. It was my first visit to New England and I was looking forward to my time of ministry there. The pastor was gracious and put me up in his home. We spent time in fellowship during the day and I found him opening his heart to me. One day as he was giving me a tour of the area we happened to drive by a graveyard. He pointed toward a row of gravestones and a story of heartache began to pour out from the depths of his heart. I discovered later that this precious minister had developed a reputation for one particular message that he shared on the teaching circuit we both traveled. This "life message" surrounded the loss of his son in a tragic automobile accident.

According to this pastor's view, his son had been far from God at the time of his death and was lost forever. His heart carried a double wound, for not only was his son gone but his eternal destiny was in question as well. I wasn't expecting his sad account. It just gushed out in a surge of pain. He hadn't asked for such tragedy. He probably had done everything he could to ensure that his son would be safe in God's arms. But none of that had worked. All that remained besides the plot of ground and a cold gravestone was the deep aching in the gut of this dear man of God.

Moments like that are exceptional. Suddenly, without asking, you're allowed to share the grief of a friend. You see beyond the surface into that realm where people carry their deepest grief in secret. Such wounds can be healed. Such aches can be relieved. There is a special physician for the soul and he's on the road with us. But for many what happens before he arrives is the final insult. As bad as the attack has been, what our lonely traveler faces now is even worse.

FIVE

ABANDONED

"They stripped him of his clothes, beat him and went away..."

It's hard to believe
That there's nobody out there
It's hard to believe
That I'm all alone

"Under the Bridge"
Red Hot Chili Peppers

Scorn has broken my heart
And has left me helpless:
I looked for sympathy, but there was none,
For comforters, but I found none.

Ps 69:20, NIV

I am forgotten by them
As though I were dead.
I have become like broken pottery.

Ps 31:12, NIV

53

I heard her during the practice set in the cavernous hall. Her raspy voice would leave a mark on my generation. More than her voice it was the sense of attack in her performance that immortalized her. I guess my musical taste or lack thereof resulted in my lack of awe over her presence.

It turned out that we both had a part on the stage that night at the Filmore Auditorium in San Francisco. She would be center stage and later on the bill. I was there at the invitation of a well-known Bay Area band who had invited me for one night of experimentation. I would accompany them on my "invention": a light organ, a miniature keyboard that was wired to a series of lights. Each note connected to a corresponding spotlight. These projected across the platform and created multi-colored shadows of the musician's bodies, dancing across the screen in rhythm behind them. It was a primitive forerunner of the modern lightshow.

Much of what happened that night is lost in the swirl of memory and drug-inspired dreams that linger somewhere in my own personal X-files. But one thing is clear. I remember sitting across from her in the overstuffed chairs and couches of the green room backstage. She was as bold and brash off stage as on. And, of course, close at hand was her seemingly ever-present flask of Southern Comfort. Here was someone at the launch point of stardom. Janice Joplin's fame and glory were growing stronger every day. But it was clear to the observing eye that she was quenching more than thirst with her little jug. Many friends and lovers would come and go, yet that bottle of amber liquid was probably closer to her in some ways than any of them.

I can't recall much of the conversation that night. She wasn't that famous yet, so I wasn't impressed. But I do remember one anecdote about her life that I came across later. It was reported that one night after a performance she made the comment that she wanted to write a song about making love to ten thousand people but going home all alone.

Loneliness. It happens, even to the famous. There's a world of celebrity and publicity all around them. They seem to be the center of attention. But they can be some of the loneliest people on planet earth.

Alone. That's where the wounded traveler found himself at the end of the assault. Such attacks are like that. Not only are you wounded and insulted, but when it's over you're all alone. I've met a lot of people like that. In fact many times they're alone because of the attack.

They're so hurt that no one wants to be around them. Janice, I'm sure, had a lot of "friends," but enough has been said about her both in fact and legend to establish that this lady was a lonely soul.

One of her contemporaries echoed these sentiments: "All the lonely people....where do they all come from."? I think I have an answer. You'll find them on the Jericho road. Beaten, broken and stripped. They rarely get up. Few help them up and if they do get up they're in such bad shape no one wants them.

Then there are guys like Sam (not his real name). He's fallen among thieves—the kind that rob you of normal passion. He's fed his soul on porn. At first such activity doesn't seem to be an assault at all. But the blows go deep and, when it's over, he's not only bruised but also pierced so deep it's hard to find the scars, let alone get medicine to them. Since his addiction to sexual fantasy, Sam's become an angry man who almost always has to have it his way. I don't think I

> *In the end, it all boils down to caring. Simple tools, but powerful medicine. This is what God has left us.*

can name one friend in his life. He's bright and talented but very hard to be around. I'm sure if I went back far enough in his life I would find lots of rejection. He's out there on the Jericho road. He's bleeding, naked and alone.

Many more join him every day. Many have never tasted drugs or illicit sex. But someone or something has left them broken. They bleed silently sometimes but still the tracks of their dissipating lives dribble through the edgy and stilted atmosphere of our 21st century world.

When you look at the final condition of the victim on the Jericho road, there appears to be little one can do to help. We're quick to blame the Levite and priest who passed by without helping but perhaps they were bewildered. Maybe their problem was not just lack of compassion but also lack of skill. How can I help this shattered person? Where do I start to put him back together? Is he still alive?

In the end, though, it all boils down to caring. There was a way to put the man back together again. Simple tools for a big problem. Simple tools, but powerful medicine. This is what God has left us. It's all found in the Good Samaritan's kit.

This book is all about using it to restore hurting people. Not every attempt will result in perfect health, but we each have an opportunity to be part of the healing process. The medicine God supplies is real. Don't be afraid to try it out. And as I heard a physician say one time, "I practice medicine." So if you need practice, there's a world of hurting people out there and God's commands are clear: "Heal the sick."

But before we open God's medicine chest we need to examine one final element of the assault: its result.

HALF DEAD

"They stripped him of his clothes, beat him
and went away, leaving him half dead."

call my name and save me from the dark
bid my blood to run
before I come undone
save me from the nothing I've become

"Bring Me to Life"
Evanessence

The beaten and broken man on the road to Jericho
was alive but just barely. He was like a zombie. His
injuries had left him stunned and comatose. Such are
many I meet on the highways of modern life. They're
there, but in a strange way they are not alive. They're animated by fear, lust, revenge and pride—but joyless. Take
away this brutal form of energy and they'd end up

depressed and lonely somewhere in an institution. Like the sad faces of those you'll find in a casino pulling the handles on slot machines while their faces remain a mask of depression. Many of them live around us. We see them every day. They appear normal on the surface but inside they're pushed along only by their egos. Some are damaged beyond repair and when I meet them my heart shutters a bit. Some of the old Hollywood B pictures come to mind. Tales of the walking dead, animated by some alien energy that's taking over the world. Scary and funny all at the same time. Sad to say, there is nothing funny about those who have been left on the road half dead; indeed there's something very scary about what happens every day to many people who wander out onto the road to play in the dangerous traffic of our modern society.

When I first met Steve (not his real name) he was part of our high school track team. He was a picture of health and a tremendous athlete. He had rugged good looks and a lithe body. He was an excellent student and the kind of guy you'd expect to end up as a teacher, executive or athletic coach. After we graduated from high school I didn't see him for several years. Then suddenly he reappeared.

At the time I was working as the assistant director of a half way house. While I was working there over a hundred men went through our rehab program. One day

Steve showed up. When I saw him I was shocked. He was extremely emaciated; he looked like a refugee from a prison camp. Even more disturbing was his mental condition. He was paranoid and distant, afraid to eat for reasons that most of us would find foolish. What strange force had changed him? Had it been a drug encounter or some genetic flaw? His case was extreme, but it's a picture of how fragile we all are.

Not long after seeing Steve again I read a story of a young Princeton student who fell into a delusional state after a stay in an eastern-style ashram. His body was reduced to a shell as he spent his days in elaborate attempts to purify himself. He would swallow long strips of gauze and then extract them in hopes of cleansing his esophagus. He died of malnutrition.

Both these men are acute pictures of the tragic problems that plagued my generation. Most of the people who trudged down the roads of the last three decades came through. But a lot of us are still the walking wounded. We found careers, got married and built families. But in moments of honesty we had to admit that part of us died out there on the highway and that we have been dragging the corpse of our hopes and dreams with us ever since. And now with the Gen X'ers and Y'ers the story goes on.

A zombie in the classic description is someone who's

been brought back from the dead and is now a slave of the one who poisoned them. Zombies lumber through haunted nights carrying out the orders of their perverted masters. They are so overcome by the effect of the strange potion that's bewitched them that they have no will of their own left. The Psalmist describes it this way.

> The enemy pursues me,
>> he crushes me to the ground;
> he makes me dwell in darkness
>> like those long dead.
> So my spirit grows faint within me;
>> my heart within me is dismayed.
>> (Ps. 143:3, 4, NIV)

A biblical proverb expands on this condition: "Like a city whose walls are broken down is a man who lacks self control" (Prov. 25:28).

A sad condition indeed. Broken and haunted by death, our lonely traveler lay waiting for time and the elements to close in and end his life. So much for the bad news—now the good news! Jesus' story is only beginning. Thankfully our story doesn't end here. There is hope for this wounded soul and it comes in a strange and unusual form. A Samaritan happens along the trail and, moved by compassion, begins the wonderful process of restoring life to the broken traveler.

SEVEN

OIL

"He went to him and bandaged his wounds, pouring in oil . . ."

I was a sailor, I was lost at sea
I was under the waves before love rescued me

"When Love Comes to Town"
Bono, U2

Oil. It flows. It soothes. Some oil is golden, as if its color displays its true worth. Pressed from olives and stored in flasks, somehow it seems to slowly seep out. Poured forth it glistens and gently settles into tranquil pools. If you had an ocean of it, you'd find few storms there. Oil keeps our machines humming along with a smooth rhythm. Oil can also heal. A few drops spread out brings comfort to ragged skin. It can be the conveyor of other balms. Blended with herbs it's transformed into an exotic topping for food. Mixed with sacred spices, it was used to anoint priests with a fragrant aroma as they carried out their holy duties. In the hands of the caring Samaritan it became medicine.

Our traveler is frayed and torn. Having been pummeled he desperately needs something which will caress. And so oil does its work, tenderizing and restoring his chaffed skin. Slowly but certainly it softens and protects. It spreads and there's not a crack or crevice that it won't fill and comfort.

What a picture of God's unconditional love! A kindness that clings to you even when you push it away. It's there, surrounding you, oozing slowly between the cracks in your soul. The world really does need it. I first began to understand it the day I came out of my own personal wilderness.

I had grown up with my share of rejection. Like many of my generation I found myself an outsider. A lot of social gatherings were painful. By the time I was in junior high, society seemed to have already assigned me my place. Because I wasn't strong or athletic I was soon firmly stuck in that land of the unpopular. This was long before the tribalism of the Gen X'ers and Y'ers. Today you have a variety of identities that hold their own charm. But not in my youth. Then your options were few: be funny, strong, terribly good looking, or be an outsider. It was lonely being an outsider. Friendless walks through the rain back from the library at night. Hours by myself, with myself, tired of myself. There were other "outsiders" then. Older students. Holy barbarians at the fringe of our culture. Intellectuals and existentialists who collected in dingy coffee houses and talked philosophy. Three years later we were hippies. Now we had our own weird but rising popularity. In a strange way we became an "in" thing.

But I soon discovered that the prejudices and cliques that had revolted me in my earlier years were just as prevalent among flower children. Even with all our talk of universal love and peace, the deeper I got into communalism the more selfishness I saw. And honestly, a lot of it was clearly emanating from my own frustrated heart. Where do you go with such discouragement?

I found it one day in the midst of a small group of college students who gathered once a week to study the Bible, pray and, most important of all, just be friends. Here I found acceptance. They all seemed to have been dressed from the same mail-order catalog, while I still bravely carried the tattered and patched rags of my hippie culture. But for whatever reason they seemed to look past all that in a way none of my fellow "drop out" friends did. There had always been a subtle chic underlying the whole counterculture anyway. From its cosmic cowboy image to its earthtone headbands and beads, there was an unspoken hierarchy of fashion and hip-ness. But I had to look hard to find it in these Christian college students with their winged tipped shoes and pressed shirts.

> *"There is no fear in love. But perfect love drives out fear."*
>
> *1 Jn. 4:18*

I couldn't shake the fact that they loved me. It was soon obvious that this love wasn't based on my fitting in to their way of dressing or acting. That wasn't why they accepted me. It was as if God was peering into my innards right through their eyes. They seemed to look deeper and I could tell it was real. All my defenses went down and I began to sense real love. Such real love dispels something from the wounded soul. It drives out insecurity. In John's epistle we read the following: "There is no fear in love. But perfect love drives out fear...." (4:18). Insecurity is a form of fear. It's remarkable how real love can dispel such anxiety.

It's amazing what insecurity can do to people. All of

us can probably remember some childhood trauma. Being embarrassed by friends. Wearing the wrong clothing to school and being ridiculed. Failing to heed one of the unwritten laws of the "in crowd" and finding yourself an outcast.

One such situation sticks out in my mind. It happened in my first year of junior high. This time of life has to be the most difficult period in our teen years. You're emerging from childhood. The little red wagon of innocence gets transformed into a street racer fueled by hormones with a speed demon at the wheel. Overnight it suddenly matters what you look like. It also matters who your friends are, what neighborhood you come from, and what the opposite sex thinks of you. You're measured by a whole new set of standards and all too often you come up lacking.

This kind of pressure causes kids to change their behavior, their dress, their grooming and for me even what I ate. My loving mother, who was into heath food before most of the world discovered the delights of yogurt and granola, made sure that she sent her son off to school with the best food she could pack away in my sack lunch. But for those who might remember the strange world of the late fifties, taking a sack lunch to school put you somewhere on the low end of the social pecking order.

As I remember, the lunch pail group ate in one area of the school cafeteria. But even in this realm I soon found myself on the outside. White bread ruled and tuna fish sandwiches or baloney-laden "Wonder Bread" were the "flavor" of the decade. My nutritious meal made me feel somewhere at the bottom of the scale.

I can still remember the reaction of my friends as I pulled my mother's treasures from the brown bag. It was a concoction of 15 grain bread and homecooked roast beef smothered in ketchup. The whole mixture weighed about two pounds. This along with some veggies, fruit and milk purchased from the lunch room menu was a nutritious meal for any growing teenager. But it just wasn't politically correct in my lunch room. My classmates took one look at this healthy mixture and their derision came quickly, spreading around my table like the pimples on my adolescent forehead. The looks said more than the words that soon followed their ghastly stares: "That's garbage. How can you eat that?" I soon found myself pushing lunch back into the brown bag and later depositing the offending object in the nearest waste can as if it were a dirty diaper.

It seems a trite thing today and perhaps insignificant, but to me it was huge. I wanted to be accepted. I didn't

want to be mocked. So that single incident began a daily rit-
ual at school. First, I started leaving my lunch bag in my
school locker. But before long it was bulging with rotting,
smelly food. I came later in the week, after school hours,
and deposited the whole mess in a nearby garbage pail. I
got caught a few times and the embarrassment forced me
to come up with a new plan. Each day on the way to school
I'd swing behind a local market and toss the offending par-
cel in a dumpster. But even there my sin found me out.
Years later someone told me that the store's meat cutter saw
my transgression and collected the wholesome package,
feeding to his heart's content on its healthy contents.

Remembering this today I'm almost tempted to ignore
its significance. But there's still a sting in its memory. Why
was I so afraid? Why was acceptance by my schoolmates
so important? I want to ask a whole generation why peer
pressure is such a strong force. Why do parents send their
kids out with healthy meals but fail to understand that
they need something else even more? They need another
food that will fortify their souls against the challenges of
a world that puts too much value on the wrong things.
There was a deep-seated need in me to be accepted.
Every teenager and adult feels this need. It may not be
embarrassment over sandwiches but it's something. Some

69

point of pressure where we feel that wedge of insecurity. Too easily we cave in and fit in. Why? Because we're insecure. Because we lack a deep and lasting sense of worth.

Experiencing such worth is oil for our wounds. Many healthy people find this cure in loving families. They find it in strong and true friendships. But many don't, and because they lack it they wander around socially and emotionally stunted. When I came to Christ I found the ultimate source of self worth. It comes from being in the presence of God. Being close to him on a regular basis has saturated my soul with the kind of love that dispels every fear. The perfect love that emanates from God's presence is real medicine. God offers such unconditional love to all of us—and especially to those who have been wounded along life's perilous trails.

Perhaps no story in the Bible illustrates this point better than Samuel's account of Prince Jonathan's son, Mephibosheth. He was the contemporary of King David, the great warrior king of Israel. David was the ultimate "jock" of his day. He had every honor a guy could want. And rightly so. He was a hero to his nation because he had stood against evil and prevailed. His trophy case was full of the gold medals of his day: the foreskins of Philistines. This guy would make some of our gridiron favorites look like wimps. Once firmly established as king, David sought to keep a covenant he had made with his fallen comrade, Prince Jonathan. He orders a search of his kingdom to find any remaining children of his former friend. "I'll be kind to your children" could be a paraphrase of the commitment David had made to his former soul mate.

Now, years later, he seeks Jonathan's children to bless them. The one surviving child, a lame and broken man, is brought before the king. He's the grandson of David's former nemeses, King Saul. We can only imagine what was going through Mephibosheth's mind as he was ushered into the king's throne room. Talk about the ultimate intimidating situation! The account found in 2 Samuel 9 is taunt with the workings of palace intrigue and the stuff of blood feuds. What will David do? Perhaps most of those around David knew little of the commitment he had made to his friend Jonathan. Perhaps even Jonathan's son was unaware of it.

Picture the scene with me. Here you are a lame, frightened man called into the presence of the absolute ruler. What do you have to offer him? What excuse can you make for your ancestor's sins against David? You're lame—a condition that happened when a nursemaid dropped you as a child. You've lived with this handicap through the years and it's shaped your worldview. You're an outcast, a weakling, a pariah. You'd never find yourself among the warriors in David's locker room joking over slain enemies and severed foreskins. You're intimidated. You pull your cloak over your shriveled feet and hope the ruler won't speak too harshly of your lack of mobility. How would King David, the man who "could run through a troop," speak to a man who hadn't walked in years? Even your name is hard to pronounce, and it comes from a clan that is no longer politically correct. And yet as you sit trembling in the presence of majesty, it's the first thing you hear. It's spoken with love and affirmation. Suddenly there's hope.

We all love to hear our name! When someone mentions it with respect we feel honored by the one who's spoken it. Imagine the honor when God speaks our name. It wasn't long after I became a Christian that I began to experience this joy. God assured me of His love in the most personal way. I realized that he was a greater King than David and yet I could sense his kindness whispering in my heart. Did I hear my name spoken verbally? No, but I heard something much deeper. Something that felt as soothing as the purest oil flowing over worn-out edges of my soul: God's presence. Such medicine began

72

the process of making me new. It's the ultimate comfort to have God honor you. To have Him speak to you with respect and genuine affection. Such reassurance is real medicine for the soul.

The next thing King David said to his subject was, "Fear not." These are the words God often speaks to those who come trembling into His presence. Compared to His glory we all come short. But there's no posturing with God. He knows who He is and who we are. He loves us and wants us to be comfortable in such a heady atmosphere.

One reason more of us aren't well is that we spend so little time in God's presence.

And so like the apostle John lying at Jesus' feet, we hear words of assurance: "Fear not." His perfect love casts out not only the terror of His majesty but every other terror.

We are to be at peace in His presence. In fact, that's what His presence brings: an overwhelming sense of peace. And those who repeatedly bask in that presence experience a deep sense of value and assurance that will help them face the mockery of peers at least and the scorn of wicked rulers at worst. David, a wise and loving

a heart to reassure his lowly subject of his safe-
much more does God desire to bring value and
re.. ..ose who find a home in His throne room.

Following King David's assurance came the invitation
to eat at the king's table for life. You're welcome here,
David says, no matter what your frailties and in spite of
the sins of your forefathers. You're welcome here. God
welcomes us the same way. He says that it doesn't matter
if you limp or even if your mother packs the wrong kind
of lunch. His covenant with His Son has made us worthy.

Once we've accepted that redemption we can dwell
with royalty and enjoy the deep security that comes from
such lofty company. Such love is unconditional. Such love
is oil to our wounds. Such love is there to bathe in. And
the more often we do, the healthier we become. One reason more of us aren't well is that we spend so little time
in God's presence. Every Christian has the privilege to
enter God's presence. There's no limit to the time we can
spend there. Mary, the sister of Lazarus, spent hours at
Jesus feet, listening to his words. But all too often we
come to God with our requests and just as quickly scurry
away to more important things, seldom realizing that what
we need to cope with a ruthless world lies in the presence of the King.

74

A picture hanging on the wall of my office illustrates this point. Several year ago my wife, Claudia, and I had the opportunity to have our picture taken with then President George Bush. One of my elders, who was a good friend of a senior congressman, was able to get us seats on the second row at a campaign stop on President Bush's short swing through California. After his brief speech we stood at the head of a large group gathered to shake the president's hand. We waited expectantly, wondering if we would have the ultimate "photo op." Reporters everywhere. Banks of video cameras. Line's of reporters. Secret Service agents that seemed as big as Goliath and not much nicer.

And then the president was there. The most powerful man in the world stopping long enough, not only to shake our hands, but to pose for a picture. He put his arm around my wife in a fatherly way. I quickly squeezed in beside her. Flash and it was all over. He had moved on to the next person in line. No matter what one's political bent, most of us are in awe of our nation's leader, whatever his party; and even if that leaves us unmoved we'd admit, if we're honest, that we're impressed by the pomp and circumstance that swirls around him.

As I look at the picture today something strikes me

about it. I notice where the president is looking. Instead of looking at the camera he's smiling at us. At first it seemed odd. But as I thought about it more, I realized what he was doing. In that short moment as he passed by in all the flurry of power, privilege and glory, his whole attention seemed to fall on us. As if we were suddenly important to him. What this fleeting moment caught on film was or might have been his attempt to close the gulf between the royalty of his position and the lowliness of ours. It seemed to say, "You guys, mister and misses Joe and Jane voter, Cal and Carla California, you're what it's all about. You're important too."

Whenever someone notices the picture in my office it usually brings a positive response. And I must admit it feels good just to recall our brief brush with "glory." It seems a little of it remains behind. As I nonchalantly tell my guest how the picture came about, my short-lived touch with American royalty bathes me again in the privilege of that day. I had access, however momentary, to Great Power and Privilege. I had access to the "Chief." What I often forget as a Christian is that this is my privilege every time I enter into a conversation with God. He is the ultimate Power. His power is beyond all others and His glory never fades. His presidency never ends and His secret service agents could wipe out an army of Goliaths. He is the CHIEF of chiefs. Hail to the Chief!

Let me press my point even more. One evening I was watching a news anchor with one of the major networks give us an insiders look at the daily operations and protocol that surrounds our nation's chief executive. It was fascinating. The reporter followed the president from his private quarters to the West Wing where the seat of power rests. We got to peek into the oval office where the world's leaders come to confer and seek favor. Such documentaries have become common and there seems to be a new one each time a new resident comes to 1600 Pennsylvania Avenue.

But no matter how many times I've seen it, I'm still amazed at how much grandeur surrounds those who hold this office for four or eight short years. Everyone around them seems to be scrambling. Well groomed and alert, these minions work tirelessly to make sure the wheels of power grind smoothly. These brilliant and talented people who scurry to do the president's bidding make the whole scene seem even more incredible. Add to that the secret service personnel, the police and military aids, especially the one who carries the black briefcase with codes and authority to launch a nuclear strike of world destroying proportions. As you watch all that it soon becomes clear why he's the most powerful man alive.

Imagine what it must be like for the ordinary citizen to be invited into this world. Somewhere in the middle of the report we catch a short vignette of the president entertaining such a family in his private quarters. It's obvious they're overwhelmed. And yet the whole time the president is at ease. And he's trying to make them feel at ease and welcome in this high and lofty place. But it's obvious that they're not, even though they seem to appreciate this privileged encounter with American "royalty." I'm sure they'll have some pictures to hang on the wall at home. Much more impressive than mine, I might add. But they'll be carrying much more than pictures back to their home. They'll be blessed with a greater sense of dignity and self worth. Their neighbors will be impressed, at least those of the same political party as the president. And they'll bathe in that glory for years. It doesn't matter how healthy emotionally and socially they already were, their stock has gone up in value. Deep down inside they know they matter to someone important and that in itself makes them secure and valued.

We've all been touched by some form of such human glory at one time or another. Perhaps it was a simple autograph of a famous person or the opportunity of front row seats at the concert of a most admired musician. Perhaps we caught a fly ball at a major league game or had a friend who became famous and they're still our friend. All of it brushes us next to splendor. But imagine with me for a moment how ordinary citizen Joe sports fan would feel if he could play ball with the "greats" or Gloria groupie if she could marry her rock star hero and live a life in the spotlight. Or if you could waltz into the oval office anytime you wanted and plead your cause with the most powerful man in the world.

Strangely enough that's what every person whom God invites into his secret place of prayer enjoys. You don't need an appointment. You just need a pure and simple heart. And the amazing thing is this: If we could get a photo of the moment, we might catch you staring into the camera; but His attention would be focused on you. The most powerful being in the universe. President Jesus is not only there to listen but he's there to share with you the deepest concerns of His heart. He's your friend. In fact He's your best friend. The writer of Psalms put it this way:. "The Lord confides in those who fear Him" (Ps 25:14). And the author of the Song of Songs takes us even deeper when he quotes the King's bride: "I am my beloved's and his desire is towards me" (Song of Solomon 7:10). This is what God offers us. The ultimate in friendship. Intimacy. Respect. Acceptance. All coming from the most powerful one of all.

What can that do to us? When we truly know the reality of such privilege, it has the power to dispel every thought of insecurity. If we ever lacked a sense of self worth, that all changes when we realize we are a valued friend of the greatest one of all. Perfect love drives out all fear. Insecurity has no place in the room with the most secure being of all. If he loves you the world can hate you and you'll still have peace. God lives in an atmosphere of total love and protection and He invites us into such a realm, not just for a brief "photo op," but for hours on end.

Time alone with God heals us. But how does it heal, and how do we spend time alone with God? For a lot of us time alone is hard enough. Add God to the equation and we're in deep decimal points. That's because our concept of God has been filtered through some religious archetype that makes God come out either a heavenly "dirty Harry" or a slightly senile but kind old grandfather. God is neither. Neither is He close to anything we can picture.

But picture this. Pick the smartest, wisest, most interesting person you'll ever meet and then throw in as much beauty, grace, and creativity as you can imagine. Then add the fact that He's not hung up on himself and that he's genuinely interested in your best as well as the good of everyone he meets. Multiply it all by a bazillion and you've got a good place to start.

When you spend time with God, do it the way some of His closest friends did. Let's take Paul and Silas as examples. Talk about wounds and abandonment! They've not only been beaten up. They've been beaten in the good, old fashioned Roman way. You know, whips, rods, and a burly jailer type with the wife-beater tunic to match. Then to top it all off, they've been thrown into the lowest part of the prison. The place where all the toilets for the other prisoners dump. And why are they there? All they've done is deliver some poor tormented damsel from wicked spirits that have been holding her hostage for most of her life. They've done good and gotten bad in return. This is a perfect place for a pity party. A great place to say, "I feel bad, I'm going to have a bad day and no one, not even God, is going to talk me out of it. In fact it's His fault and until He gets me out of this mess I'm just going to sit here and stew in this cauldron of human excrement and my own foul temper."

No, they're not about to do that because they know God. They know His character, His love for them and, most of all, they know He has a way of taking even the most difficult situation and turning it on its end for His glory. I can almost picture their response. "Well, here we are with unlimited time to pray. Let's find out what God's up to."

Joyfulness is a great healer. Fear runs from its presence because God dwells at the center of all true joy.

It starts like most conversations with God should, with thanks and praise for who God is and what He's done. Soon songs are rolling off their lips from some place deep beneath their bruised ribs. This session with God is not about to end with a fellowship time and shaking-hands-with-your-neighbor-type ending like many of our church gatherings. No, God shows up. I mean really shows up. Perhaps it was like the old preacher used to preach it. The song service was so good that not only were the angels tapping their feet but God started tapping His as well. The earth shook, the prison doors flew open and the prisoner's chains fell off.

Now the tables have turned. The jailer's the one who's depressed. So much so that he's about to take his life.

Paul and Silas bring him the gospel and soon he's rejoicing as his whole family gets saved. Now the former torturer is washing his prisoners' wounds and finding his own inner ones healed in the process. The whole atmosphere is charged with healing. The church in Philippi has just grown by several members, Paul and Silas have found some new friends and God's character has once again been vindicated. How? All because these apostles spent time in God's presence, reflecting on His glory instead of focusing on their own hurts and sorrows.

Circumstances will often force us to dwell in the broken places. But learning to rejoice is key to healing. You come into God's presence and soon the oil of gladness is flowing. Insecurity has a way of fleeing in such an atmosphere. Some of the greatest moments of healing in my life have come from sessions of laughter and joy. Joyfulness is a great healer. Fear runs from its presence because God dwells at the center of all true joy.

Paul wrote these same Philippians from another jail and prescribed the very medicine he no doubt was treating his own soul with: "Rejoice in the Lord always, and again I say rejoice" (Phil 4:4). Try it. Soon prison walls will crumble, chains will fall away and angels will come and pour oil in your wounds. Fear finds no quarter in the presence of joy and rejoicing. Insecurity melts away when the soul looks up to God and chooses to laugh.

An incident from one of my dearest friend's early days of ministry perfectly illustrates this great truth. He had recently come to America and joined the staff of an inner city ministry. Often his assignments took him to dangerous neighborhoods at the wrong time. On one such occasion he was walking back to the ministry center. Picture the scene with me. A long New York city block in the wrong part of town. A distant streetlight casts long shadows. Crumbled cigarette packages and old ding-dong wrappers are pushed through the gutters on a fetid breeze. Barred doors and broken window panes stared down on the street like the blackened eyes of old pirates who've seen one too many throats slit. My friend is trying to get home before his gets slit.

That hope is soon threatened by two sinister characters more gruesome than pirates. They press towards him apparently to mug or murder. What will our lonely traveler do now? Certainly not fight his way out. In those days he was about as skinny as I was in my 20's. He's left with few choices. Trust God or die. Or Trust God *and* die.

Now the tension increases. The thieves press closer, intent on their evil deed. Our skinny minister reaches somewhere into the depth of his soul and finds the courage to drive away the demons both natural and supernatural with the one weapon that all of them fear—praise to God from a joyful heart. In an instant the skinny victim is transformed into a praising machine. He spins around to the surprise of his assailants and with shouts of praise he fills the night air with Hallelujahs. Now it's the muggers who are in terror. They are suddenly stopped in their tracks, trapped by a barrage of thanks to God. They have only one way out. Back the way they've come. They retreat and none too quickly as the unseen winds of heaven carry tormenting echoes of praise whispering in their ears long after they turned the first corner.

Fear cannot live in the atmosphere of praise. Insecurity can find no home where God is glorified. As we spend time reflecting God's goodness and joyfully thanking Him for it, we leave such a place more complete than when we came into it. We leave it with the deepest part of us assured, comforted and saturated with peace.

So it is. God invites us to wait in His presence, to bask in his love and to draw all we need from it. Such oil will heal the deepest wound. Such Therapy, if applied often enough, will secure what has been pierced and broken. The bruised will be made whole with the salve of heaven.

EIGHT

WINE

*"He went to him and bandaged his wounds,
pouring in oil and wine."*

People always take a step away from what is true
that's why I like you around.

"I Want You"
Third Eye Blind

The truth is like wine. Funny you say, alcohol and honesty? Well, sometimes we get more truth from a drunk than a sober parson. Having been a minister for some thirty-odd years I can say that. A lot is held back under the banner of wisdom and restraint. No such luck with the inebriated. Once the inhibitions are lowered, bang! Out comes what's inside. But as most of us know, telling the truth involves much more than spilling out one's uncensored thoughts. Therefore when I say truth and wine are alike, I'm speaking more to the medicinal aspects of both.

The lonely traveler needed medicine. Strong medicine, applied to the right place. Wine is strong medicine. The Samaritan did not use it to numb the pain. In fact, in this act of healing, the pain was actually increased. The wine was not poured into the man's mouth but into his opened wounds. Ouch! How could such an act be mercy? To understand how, I'd like to go back to an incident in my own childhood.

I grew up in a small college town in the Sacramento valley. I was about twelve and our idyllic city was in the midst of a long hot summer. Temperatures often soared well above 100 in mid July, and could hover there for days. But young lads like me had found one way to escape the repressive heat—a favorite of boys since the days of Tom Sawyer. With central air conditioning still a relatively new development, the local swimming hole offered a welcome break. I was on my way there when a most painful incident occurred. Today people laugh when I tell this story. But it wasn't funny then, I promise you.

Here's the picture: a band of boys, heady with the

freedom of summer, on their way to a day of aquatic escape. Spielberg could film this just the way it happened. We're all on our bikes, racing along in the heated morning air, naked, except for our swimming trunks. Loose change jangled in our pockets and pictures of high dives and high fives pranced in our youthful heads. Add one more typically Spielbergian touch. As the wheels race around and the bike pedals pump, the camera moves in on one that has a loose kickstand. With each rotation there's an annoying click as the pedal strikes a loose brace. It's irritating to half the senior citizens on the block. "Why doesn't the silly kid get his bike repaired? The noise is ruining my morning paper reading."

Not today. On we pedal, dreams of chilling bliss driving us forward. Racing, our pace increases. And of course who needs to hold onto the handlebars? Our hands are free, waving away with enthusiasm.

Like a blur we pass the last house near the field where we'd spent days digging foxholes and fighting imaginary Nazis. Again, picture it with me. Tanned legs flashing, lean arms, free from the restraints of steering, pumping up and down, almost as if we'd stopped biking and started running in midair. And then in an instant I was in the air, launched there by the force of my own pedaling. The kickstand popped loose, the pedal stopped, frozen in place, and all 80 pounds of me went over the handlebars and onto the pavement. And then my bike followed me down, twisting, spinning and trapping me in its chrome metal vise.

It hurts even thinking about it. I can still recall the terror in my voice. At this point there was only one place of comfort and healing. Home was back up the street the way I'd come. But this time I limped and ran without my bike, seeking the mercy of my mom.

As I turned the corner onto our street my fellow Tom Sawyers had already brought her the news. She gently led me into the house and then lovingly into the bathroom. Bidding me sit on the toilet seat, she began what every mother who's ever helped an "owie" knows well. She began the painful process of cleaning my wounds. "No Mom, not the methiolate." For those who didn't grow up in the 50's, let me explain. This strange "healing" substance, concocted, no doubt, by a sadist, was what you used in my younger days to kill the bacteria in a wound. The pain it produced was greater than the wound itself. It seemed to have a way of penetrating every cell that was suffering and then added an even greater terror. Mercifully, modern medicine has come up with better ways of dealing with bacteria.

All real medicine hurts in some way. The surgeon cuts to heal, the bone often must be painfully moved to be set, and the aching tooth must be pulled or drilled to bring wholeness again. The wine poured into the lonely traveler's wounds was doing its job. The alcohol in it was killing the bacteria. But it wasn't pleasant being on the receiving end of such compassion. Healing has a way of hurting some-

One thing I learned for sure: if I want to be whole, I have to listen to the truth.

times. So does truth. I can almost hear you saying, "Bring on the wine, only this time pour it down my throat to numb the pain."

Back to the scene in my mother's bathroom. I objected loudly, but she completed the procedure. I was finding more than loving arms and comforting words. In the middle of all my pain I was finding love, love that was painful but love that heals. It was the kind of love we all need if we're ever to be truly whole.

Truth hurts. And it seems to hurt even more if you're already wounded.

But truth also heals. Many times we only want the oil,

not the wine, and not the binding that will hold it there until it's done its work. One thing I learned for sure: if I want to be whole, I have to listen to the truth. I didn't want my mom's medicine, but wisdom held me there and so did she. I've met many people who haven't found wholeness because they won't hold still for the truth. It's too painful.

In my own life, God still seems to bring me, after 30-plus years as a minister, face to face with this kind of pain. Too many times I've run from it and stayed sick. But each time I've held still and let the truth burn its way into my soul I've found therapy. Why did God make something so helpful so agonizing? I don't have the answer to that but I know if you can stand this kind of hurt, it will eventually heal the deeper hurt.

So many people refuse this kind of therapy. They think it's not true compassion. In my years of counseling and working with broken people, I found that this is one of the biggest stumbling blocks to wholeness. The "bacteria" of self, sin, and evil thrives in our broken places and unless we deal with it, as painful as the process is, it will not only stay there, but it will thrive there. Pour in all the oil you want. Bind up the gash, but under the bandages sickness goes on spreading until the whole body is sick.

Gangrene in its final stages has only one solution—amputation. So take your medicine and be whole.

The writer of Proverbs leaves us this confirmation of the dual power of oil and wine: "By mercy and *truth* is iniquity purged" (Prov. 16:6 KJV). You need more than the comfort of oil's unconditional warmth to be complete. You need the Truth. There's something about an honest rebuke that brings completeness. Proverbs 27:5, 6 says, "open rebuke is better than secret love." The truth told openly and wisely will correct something that all the gentleness and tenderness in the world will never heal. To be healed something has to be corrected. Something sick has to be removed, and in doing so we often want to strike the one who's bringing the healing.

Here's a secret. Listen, even when it hurts. Listen, when it hurts your pride. Listen, when its goes against the way you see the world. Listen, and don't reject the one who pours in the medicine.

Successful people listen to those who don't agree with them all the time. Jerome Hines, the famous opera singer, used to pay a coach big money by the half hour just to point out his vocal failures. Have you ever considered this? Does Tiger Woods listen to his trainer? You better believe he does. Is his trainer a better golfer? It's doubtful;

but he has one thing the famous golfer lacks, a different perspective. He has some information that Tiger can't see. Most people who become great in sports, business and life have done so by listening to those who point out their weak spots, their less than whole places. It's painful but it heals. Pride might keep you from listening but if you want wholeness you'd better.

Here's an additional thought. Should you decide to bring truth to people, listen closely. It's the way you tell the tale that makes all the difference. The Apostle Paul puts it like this, "speaking the truth in love, we'll grow up..." (Eph 4:15). It was love that kept me in my mother's makeshift infirmary. I knew she really cared for me. The lonely traveler, through the fog of his pain, must have known that the Samaritan was a healer. Perhaps lying there on the ground receiving this pain-filled mercy was unbearable, but sensing the kindness of the man kept him in a posture of receiving. If you haven't found your Samaritan yet, find one soon. Better yet, be one to someone else.

Everyone needs someone to tell him the truth. That's the nature of true brotherhood. Marriages where husband and wife listen to the tender but honest correction of their spouses stay healthy and happy. Partnerships without truth fester and swell with emotional infection. Again, it's so important how you bring the truth to those who need it. Words spoken in love are much more likely to be received.

What is it about this "speaking the truth in love"? It has a lot to do with the motive of the teller. A story emerges from the files of Elisha the prophet. A mighty Syrian warrior comes to his door for healing. He's a leper but he's also rich and powerful. He's brought a considerable bounty with him and is prepared to pay grandly for real health. Elisha doesn't even come out to meet him and his entourage. He simply commands him to go and wash in the humble Jordan River.

But Naaman will have none of it. He's from a better country with better and bigger rivers. His pride simply won't allow him to take the cure. After a brief verbal exchange, his wise servant ends up persuading his master to take his medicine. After seven humiliating dips in the lowly river of the Hebrews, the great general comes up clean. The point is this: the servant knew what his master needed. He knew the truth and finally convinced his leader to listen to it. The wisdom in this situation lies in the motive of the servant. He loved his master and wanted him whole. Before we can be healers we need to truly love. And before we can often receive healing, we must know that the bearer of the message really loves us.

Wine is made from fruit that has been crushed, stored and aged until it changes into a special substance that can deal with infection. As I said earlier, poured down our throats it has one effect, poured into our wounds another. Wine is stored in skins. God stores His precious truth in our vessels. Truth must have time to age within us. The wineskin must age with the wine. Eager young ministers filled with truth are often filled with themselves as well. The wine is poured out before its time. Truth is truth. But for anyone who's heard a skilled and mature Christian share God's word effectively and then heard someone unskilled in the Bible try the same thing, the difference is apparent.

Facing the truth of forgiveness brings release from the death that lurks in untreated wounds.

Infections come easily. They're borne on the air and carried on our skin. Our outer man can handle them. But once there's a breech in our protective membrane, microbes become dangerous. Left unconfronted, they become poison. One of the most deadly of these bacteria is unforgiveness. Most of the people I've met who have been wounded carry with them deep places of unforgiveness. Someone's hurt them badly and long after the blow has been delivered its effect remains in the form of germs that grow, decaying everything around them. Left untreated, the sickness will consume limb and then life. Thankfully there is a way to overcome such a noxious illness.

God's medicine will burn its way into such sickness and if allowed to stay will remove deadly micro organisms. It takes courage and a willingness to face the truth. In Matthew 18 Jesus brings his remedy to bear in a unique story. In this parable we discover a servant who owes a massive debt to his king. In desperation the debtor begs for mercy and promises to repay. The king, moved with compassion, forgives the debt. But the forgiven man goes out and finds someone who owes him money. Like the king he also demands repayment. His debtor promises to repay, only asking for time. But his pleas go unheeded. No mercy is given. The very man the king had previously forgiven casts his debtor into prison. When the king hears of this travesty he reacts quickly. He reinstates the debt and instructs his servants to cast the ungrateful and selfish servant into a place of torment until all his debt is paid. Jesus closes this story with this profound declaration. "So likewise shall my heavenly father do also unto you, if you from your hearts forgive not every one his brother their trespasses."

Facing the truth of forgiveness brings release from the death that lurks in untreated wounds. With time the ache of such sorrow is forgotten. The classic example is found in the story of Joseph. He was a man with big dreams. A man whose naiveté seemed as big as his imaginings. He seemed to completely misunderstand his brothers' bitterness toward him. This was one dream that seemingly never entered his mind. But his older siblings were up to no good. And when they finally found the opportunity, they stripped him of his robe, tossed him into a pit and eventually sold him into slavery.

His plight is somewhat similar to our lonely traveler. Taken down to Egypt he soon begins to prosper. Through a series of intrigues he eventually finds himself second only to Pharaoh over all of the land of his exile. Later, when his famished brothers come seeking food from Pharaoh's storehouses, they fail to recognize their now powerful brother. Although hints of bitterness remain in Joseph, it's apparent that the major issue has been settled. He has forgiven them years before. The clue to this lies in the name of his firstborn son, Mannasseh. Mannasseh means "to forget." God had made him forget his toil and all his father's house.

You can't forget until you forgive. God helps us forget when we have forgiven. I can remember painful times in my life, but the sting that went with them is gone. It was removed years ago in the mystery of God's love. But I can promise you that had I held onto the old hurt by failing to forgive, I would still be in torment today. I've met people who carry hurts half a century old. War veterans who still hate and broken people who won't forget injustice that struck them in their youth. If you sit with them long enough, their lists of accusations and bitter words tumble out. It seems to come from a deep well churning within. A sea of torture that won't let them rest. How the truth would set them free from such anguish. But that would first require another kind of pain: the sting of truth, painful but much less severe in the long run. Compared to decades of grief it would seem as insignificant as a needle prick. When God brings such medicine to our soul will we receive it? The lonely traveler did and it was an important part of his way to recovery.

God has poured His wine into my wounds many times. Sometimes I've found myself reacting to it. I haven't always known how to deal with the offense that truth brings. Years ago when we lived in Northern California, we bought a home on the typical suburban cul-de-sac. We were the last ones to move into the neighborhood and initially found those living around us friendly. One man who lived two houses away was on our door step the day we first saw the house. He offered us his business card. He was an insurance salesman. We soon found our new environment nice but socially cold. Each house was fitted with a steel roll-up garage door on a remote control. I'd be working out in the yard and hear my neighbors' garage opening even before I saw their car. They'd pull into the garage, the door would close behind them and they disappeared without so much as a hello.

Our salesman neighbor turned out to be somewhat fastidious. He kept his own driveway and much of the asphalt in front of his home hosed neatly down. We proceeded to landscape our yard soon after we moved in except for one small area to the left of the drive. It remained filled with fist-sized dirt clods and a few weeds. One day after returning from church, and in a particular state of spiritual saturation, I found myself confronted with a note left on my door by my neat neighbor. He stated his displeasure with my son. Apparently he'd been lobbing dirt clods into the center of the asphalt circle in front of our homes. It seemed that my son's projectiles were leaving ugly brown spots everywhere.

Well, all of my spiritual saturation dried up quickly. I began rehearsing the litany of complaints I was about to make concerning my neighbor son's failings when I felt the wine of the truth rushing into my offended heart. It went something like this: "Overcome evil with good. Return blessing for cursing. Be slow to anger" (Rom. 12:17, 1 Thess. 5:15, 1 Peter 3:9). It was not something I wanted to hear. In fact, the instructions that came with it were plain: "Go ask forgiveness for your son's handy work." This is not what I wanted to hear at the moment, but I soon found myself outside my neighbor's door knocking sheepishly, while I stood in the glare of his porch light and stared up at the peep hole, the whole time imagining him behind it, staring back at me and preparing his accusations.

Was I surprised at his response after he opened the door with a kind hello and I managed to squeeze out an apology! To my delight he invited me in and for the first time since I lived on this cul-de-sac, we began a relationship-building conversation.

It may seem like a silly incident, but such tiny offenses often turn into major ones, embittering and dividing people for life. Like the man who was offended when his wife brought home too much sugar from the store. Not only did he get mad but he stayed mad for forty years. His unforgiveness reached such heights that he finally sawed their house in two, boarding up the open halves and eventually moving his wife's portion to another part of their property. Such a lifetime of pain could have been avoided if he'd just borne the brief pain of the truth of forgiveness. It would have hurt to humble himself, but not nearly as much as the hurt he would carry for the rest of his life.

God's wine is good medicine and the sooner it's applied the better. Small infections can be cured quickly when one embraces the truth.

NINE

BINDING UP THE WOUNDED

"And he bound up his wounds...."

A year ago you crashed on this bridge right here
But we can run back home today,
You were made that way

"In the Broken Places"
David Wilcox

Several years ago our son was diagnosed with a cancerous tumor in his thigh. His doctor told us that surgery and radiation offered the best hope for Jonathan's recovery. I can still remember my deep feelings of concern as we prayed with him before going into surgery. He would be placing his body under the knife of a gifted and compassionate man. But still this instrument of healing would cut and penetrate his flesh. And once the work was done the cut would have to be closed.

Our lonely traveler had fallen under no such mercy. The blows of his assailants did great damage. Blunt clubs and sharp knives had opened deep gashes in his flesh. His life flowed steadily from these breaks. There could be only one remedy: binding.

When my son emerged from surgery his thigh was wrapped in layers of gauze. Later, once it was removed, a row of staples was revealed firmly holding the flesh together where the surgeon's scalpel had cut its probing path. Days later I watched as the surgeon quickly and deftly removed each metal clip with a nifty little tool designed for such work. Ah, the wonders of modern medicine! They cut you up and then they staple you up. Our ancient Bible doctor had no such technology. But somewhere, either from his saddlebags or from his own clothing, long strips of cloth would be taken to bind up the wounds.

Binding sometimes can mean bondage. To some the thought of restriction carries with it images of prison, chains and repression. But to the wounded, binding means healing. The Samaritan, once he has poured in his medicine, took strips of cloth and gently but firmly drew them across the jagged gashes in the hurting traveler's flesh. Once they were in place the healing could begin. Wounded patients rarely leave the doctor's presence without some suture or bandage.

I've had the privilege of traveling to remote villages in Africa on missions of mercy and I've watched while the medical team from my church binds up the wounded. I've seen those hurting people, whose gauze-covered appendages testify to loving and proper medicine, walk away from such treatment thankful but with new restrictions. They know that days if not weeks of this regimen will be necessary to complete their healing. And yet they accept their new limitations with a sense of grateful resolve. This should be the case for those who carry wounds of the soul. But often it's not.

I've never broken a bone in my body but I learned something from observing the trauma of some of my fellow schoolmates in years past. I saw that once a bone had been shattered a cast and immobility soon followed. And even though it meant restriction and limitation for awhile, my youthful friends accepted their plaster and cloth nooses almost as a badge of honor. They held them out to be signed and displayed as a testament to their courage. But beneath the plaster prison encasing their broken member healing was taking place. But for the healing to be complete the broken parts had to be held firmly in place. Likewise cuts and gashes must be sown up and kept without stress to heal. And such is the nature of inner healing.

One wounded soul sat in my office a few years ago. Let's call him Jason. He was in the midst of the break up of his marriage. This was not his first divorce. It was evident that he was repeating a pattern. He was in pain and he needed real medicine. Oil, wine and something else. Christian community. Such a society not only serves as the conduit for God's medicine, it also provides the firm wrappings to hold broken places in check. It keeps us from opening old wounds with foolish behavior. Such was the case with Jason. Once we had poured in the oil and wine, my counsel was simple, "Stay related. Stay accountable." To break the old pattern he needed the gashes in his heart sown up. He needed bands of love to firmly hold him in place so healing could take place.

I've seen this work many times. Whether it's a half-way house or a 12-step program, I've seen its effectiveness. Often its in the environment of loving but accountable groups meeting in small settings. These "communities" do something souls alone can't do. They serve as the bandages that hold our wounded places together until they begin to heal. They served as the covering to hold the medicine against our innards until it's accomplished its work.

The apostle Paul in his letter to the Galatians instructs them to restore those who had fallen morally. In kindness they were to provide an atmosphere of accountability and structure where broken people could heal. "If any see his brother overtaken in a fault, you which are spiritual restore such a one in a spirit of meekness, considering your own selves lest you also be tempted" (Gal. 6:1).

There's a key for us in the word restore. The Greek word from which it's taken contains the concept of the type of healing that a bone goes through when it is knit together. Restoration requires layers of firm but tender boundaries. Christian communities can provide this. It provides a place where each person committed to the best for us can be another layer of answerability. Soft like a bandage against the skin but firm enough to hold us in place until what has been torn open can be mended.

My first years in the community of Christ provided me with a loving but "in my face" environment. The temptations to go back to the lifestyle that had left me wounded were many. And even though my heart had clearly found a strong and new focus, there could be moments of weakness when the old wounds might break open. But now I had loving people holding me in place.

Years later I still find such boundaries surrounding me. But those who hold them there are wise, and years of healing have left a "new" memory. The old wounds are pale blue now and deep beneath the surface. The broken places have grown back together but they ache sometimes and when stressed seem to want to break along the old lines. But then thankfully the bandages are close by to strengthen and restore me once again.

> *Once you've embraced the oil and wine, make room for the loving boundaries God puts in your life.*

It was months before my son completely recovered from the long gash and the radiation treatment that followed. The cancer's gone now. Slowly and surely movement began again. He went from crutches to limping. From walking, to running, to playing in the surf. Gradually freedom came back and health was restored. But it took time. Time under the firm orders of the doctor. Times of immobility and restriction. But time, as often has been

BINDING UP THE WOUNDED

said, is a great healer. So once you've embraced the oil and wine, make room for the loving boundaries God puts in your life. Allow His Word and the community of His Son to do their work of healing even if they seem to gently bind at times.

My first four years of ministry found me in a Christ-centered half-way house where I served as an assistant director. My wife and I worked with dozens of young men who had come to Christ and were emerging from a lifestyle of drug and alcohol abuse. We saw God at work there as many of them began to heal mentally and emotionally. But as part of this routine we also saw how important restrictions and accountability were. These men needed limits. They needed loving confines to hold them from stepping back into their old patterns. They needed accountability to surround them until the broken places could be healed.

Sometimes such limits can seem almost abusive, but more often than not they're an important first step towards wholeness. Like bandages around a wound, so are relationships maintained with accountability.

Most people don't go through the type of crises that the young men we worked with experienced, but we all need accountability in our lives if we want to see healing. Twelve step groups have worked so well because they recognize this principle. If people know that they're going to have to report their actions and choices to someone else, they tend to move away from temptation. Also when such "bandages" are administered in love you have an additional element of healing.

No doubt the Samaritan applied more than one treatment and those who later took his place continued the process. God's community is a lot like that. We're here to support, comfort, warn and exhort one another toward proper conduct. Many a "spiritual giant" has fallen simply because he had no bandages of love to bind up a broken place in his life.

One of my dear friends who came out of the counter-culture shortly after I did had a moment when he fell back into his old selfish patterns. He had experienced some sudden emotional rejection and out of reaction began to take drugs again. It was evident that such action also opened him up to the evil spiritual forces that had possessed him before his conversion. His roommate at the time was a strong Christian. Once he became aware of my friend's problem he gently but firmly guided him back. He not only showed him love but also refused to let him rationalize his actions and head down the old paths. My friend later described the experience. It was as though he saw Jesus walking across stormy waters to bring him to safety.

All of us need such bandages. We need the firm and loving restrictions that will keep us in check. We need something to act as temporary support until we find inner strength. Many church leaders use this same principle to restore fallen ministers. They are removed from ministry for a season until what is broken can be mended. Gradually, as their spiritual, emotional and mental health is restored, the restrictions are gradually removed and they are allowed under the guidance of a senior minister to resume their ministry once again. I've seen the successes of those who've submitted to this process. I've also seen the failures of those who've rejected it, stating that such requirements are too confining or legalistic. There was a good reason why the Samaritan bound his patient's wounds, and there are still good reasons today.

TEN

THE INN

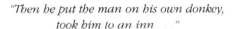

"Then he put the man on his own donkey,
took him to an inn . . ."

You'll be given love
You'll be taken care of
You'll be given love
You have to trust it

"All Is Full of Love"
Bjork

A white fog lay like a heavy silk over his mind. Here and there tiny pinpricks pushed their way into his psyche. Then the blessed numbness of unconsciousness gradually retreated in the face of his pain. Slowly he emerged into the real world again. He had faintly been

113

aware of the mercy he'd received on the road hours earlier. The soothing oil and the searing sting of the wine had brought strange assurance each time they woke him from his stupor. There had been a bumpy but hopeful ride on a lowly beast of burden. Then he'd overheard snatches of conversation from a wizened and gentle innkeeper. Now the warmth of a plain but sturdy bed hugged him with its comfort. We can only guess what the man thought as he emerged from the stupor of his roadside terror. The scriptures say that the Samaritan "took care of him." Perhaps the scene unfolded something like this.

A face appeared through the fog of his coma. It came and went in the midst of soothing acts of nurture. It watched him hopefully as firm but gentle hands spooned broth into his mouth. Words of assurance were soon followed by more kindness. Gradually questions formed. Who was this stranger? What had motivated this seraph of compassion?

Was he a fellow Jew? A merchant or pilgrim on his way to the holy city? Was he one of the many religious leaders that frequented the ancient highway to the temple city? Could he be the innkeeper's servant, hoping for extra income from the wounded pilgrim once he'd revived? As he became more aware of his surroundings the identity of his rescuer slowly began to emerge. His caregiver's accent had the odd and uncomfortable ring of the region north of Jerusalem. The cut of clothing and color of the fabric clearly spoke of the ethnic uniqueness of his nurse. The man was a Samaritan.

A sudden rush of repulsion surged in him. He wanted to push his nurse away. He wanted to shout out his indignity. Jews had no relations with the Samaritans. Why would such a man stop for him? The breach between their ancestors had been too great for time to heal. The bitterness his people held against this mixed race was momentous. Their ancestors had intermarried with pagan settlers and developed a perverted and compromised teaching, building their own religious system. They claimed to worship the way God truly commanded and they prided themselves in such religious convictions. These were people you didn't talk to, much less ask for a favor.

And now such a man was caring for him. Samaritans were beneath him. Yet as the mercy continued and he faced the reality of who was caring for him, the incredible contrast of his prejudice and this man's acts of kindness collided. Perhaps he had been wrong to categorize this race as evil. Perhaps he'd built his aloof thinking on the wrong ideas. Now he must face his helper and be thankful? It was time to overlook all the years of rivalry and bitterness. Now he must do the unthinkable. He must include another race, another creed into his world. His world must get bigger.

The inn is a lot like church. It's a place where there are many travelers. Some are resting from a weary journey. Others are feeding and refreshing the fatigued travelers. Some are in a state of repair, others sharing stories of the road around a table spread with food. Such travelers come

If you want to be part of God's healing community, you have to learn social, cultural, and ethnic flexibility.

from many backgrounds, but they all must share the comfort of the public house together. To stay here you must be willing to share it with others.

A few days after I had my life-changing encounter with Christ, an eager and sincere college student who had been praying for me for some time took me to church. Now that I'd begun the Christian life, he wanted to make sure I was firmly planted in a good Christian community. The church he chose was unique. It was not the big con-

116

gregation in the right neighborhood but a small fellow-ship on the other side of the freeway.

It was a happy place filled with young couples with small children and a collection of older "saints" who knew how to "pray you through." One of its outstanding characteristics was its cultural flavor. It was definitely Midwestern. "Oakie." The singing was lead by a balding man with a giant grin. He accompanied himself on an old electric guitar. This slice of Americana was different for a California-raised hippie who'd never seen grits and certainly never had biscuits and gravy for breakfast. Along with this cultural Middle American stew came a sincere aroma of kindness and concern. Still, it took a lot of getting used to. But that little family of believers was just what the doctor had ordered. I had to practice the virtue of laying aside my own social and ethnic prejudices and experience the life of Christ coming through vessels that appeared odd and a little square to say the least.

If you want to be part of God's healing community, you have to learn social, cultural, and ethnic flexibility. When Paul writes the Ephesians in his profound letter he stresses that there's something each member brings to the mix. There's some special ingredient that God has put in these vessels he chooses to minister to one another.

117

Without them you won't be complete. We need each other regardless of our styles, tastes and racial backgrounds (Eph. 4:11-16).

The fellowship I pastor in San Diego has a cultural and ethnic mix that reflects diversity both socially and economically. Although we're located in an affluent suburb, we have members from Africa, Asia, Europe and Latin America. I personally delight in this cultural salsa. There's a certain spice there that speaks of people laying aside their differences for a higher cause.

The Samaritan reached beyond his own religious ghetto. His actions should be an example to all of us. "Who is my neighbor?" the lawyer asked. Perhaps he was hoping that love could be expressed in some safe place. But Jesus used the act of this religious "low life" to dramatize the sort of courage God calls us to when we seek to love like He does.

Now that the wounded traveler was emerging from his pain and recognized who his deliverer was, he must also make the choice to lay aside his prejudice and cultural hang ups and make connection with the unknown.

I found genuine love and truth in the quaint little community of believers I joined as a young Christian. I saw them reach out and not only embrace me but many others who were different from them. I can still remember my pastor embracing one of my wilder friends who came through the door of the church house. He came in barefoot; his hair was long and curly, appearing as if he'd just stuck his finger in a light socket. Shocking! But my dear pastor unashamedly wept for that confused hippie who wandered into the fellowship that day.

Yes, it was a stretch for me but it was even more of one for all of these "square" folks who took us in and spoke truth to us until our broken places began to heal. I came away from my years in that little church with the sort of social health that has allowed me to embrace and minister to a diversity of people over the years. I have ministered on five continents to people from many different social and economic backgrounds. In every place the lessons of the past have helped me reach out to those who are different from me.

I believe that the lonely traveler not only found physical healing in that inn but also a whole new understanding of who his neighbors really were. Now he had a choice. He could either continue in his old ways or follow in the footsteps of his healer. He had the opportunity to become a healer as well. Jesus put it this way: "So which of these three do you think was neighbor to him

119

who fell among the thieves?" (Luke 10:36). Jesus is still asking this question today. He's asking us to step beyond our narrow social, cultural, ethnic and economical restrictions and open up to others. Who are the Oakies or hippies in your life?

Maybe you're like the guy in the movie "My Big Fat Greek Wedding" who has to make that cultural leap to connect with someone he really loves. We all have areas in our lives like this where God is calling us to grow. It may not be hippies and square folks, but the gap is still there and God is calling you to build a bridge over it to those who are different. There's something out there in each member of God's family that you need. It's the love and truth in God's first aid kit.

The Samaritan brought the wounded man to this place to rest and heal. He paid for his stay—two silver coins paid to the innkeeper. And here is one parallel that must not be overlooked. Ultimately, the Samaritan is a picture of Jesus. He's the one who finds us out on the lonely highway. He binds up our wounds and carries us to safety and it's He who purchases our stay at the ultimate place of recovery. His Father runs the inn. It's a place where saints and seeking sinners find food, shelter and restoration.

The lonely traveler was broke. All he possessed had been taken. He retained not one shekel left to buy his way into this bed and breakfast place. But the Samaritan had it covered. But at what price?

Silver coins speak of redemption. But like the lonely traveler none of us can pay for it. We're broke, morally and spiritually. The Bible puts it this way:

Jesus purchased our stay at the ultimate place of recovery. His Father runs the inn.

"When we were yet without strength Christ died for the ungodly" (Rom. 5:6). His sacrificial death purchased our healing. The prophet Isaiah proclaimed it like this "by his wounds we were healed" (Isaiah 53:5). Jesus knows what it's like to be wounded. His own suffering not only allowed him to experience the human condition and therefore have great empathy for us, His suffering actually heals us. From his wounds flowed life giving blood. It was the evidence of a life given in sacrifice and the release of a healing force. Just as a blood transfusion can restore health to those who receive it, so Christ's blood restores us. It's a reality. The Scriptures say that the life of the flesh is in the blood (Lev. 17:11). God's life is in the blood of His son Jesus. His blood carries away the sin that infects us and brings the nutrients of a new nature. Such substance builds the cells of our soul. Its life clears our conscience and lifts the guilt that defiles our hearts and minds.

The parable tells us that the Samaritan carried the wounded man on his own beast of burden. Even so when Jesus found me beaten and wounded on my Jericho road I couldn't move. He lifted me up and switched places with me. I was carried along by a grace I didn't possess. Such is God's mercy to each one of us. Christ tasted death that we might live forever. He switched places with us. He became sin that we might become righteous (2 Cor 5:21). It's this heart of love that marks the life of Jesus. He walked so we might ride. He gave that we might receive.

Sad to say, though, we're not merely victims. Each one of us have wounded others. In some way and some time each of us have been thieves. We robbed someone of love or wounded others with our words and actions. We were part of a gang that left a soul alone on the roads of this life. We therefore need Christ to heal us, too. We need his blood to remove the guilt and erase the oppression from our souls.

He also calls us into the unique position that the

innkeeper found himself in. He left us payment. Two silver coins called grace and love, and he asks us to give ourselves to the ongoing restoration of those around us who've been wounded.

The very fact that the Samaritan left money behind for the ongoing care of his patients speaks to the fact that healing takes time. God calls us to be patient with others. To work with them until healing is final. People start with crutches and it's often weeks and months before they walk freely. Sometimes it's years before they run. But healing will come.

The Samaritan promised to return. So will Christ. He's looking to find the lonely traveler restored and also to see how those who were to care for him have spent his silver. Their job was to take care of the wounded as he had. To restore those who'd faced the terror of the "Bloody Way." I'm certain it's His hope that they've done their job with the same compassion and understanding he displayed.

It's been almost 2000 years since Jesus gave us this wonderful parable. He's still bringing people to the Inn. If you're one of those broken trekkers I encourage you to check in today. The rent's already been paid and there are a bunch of us who would gladly make room for you.

Notes

Chapter 1
*Bob Dylan, "Highway 61 Revisited," *Highway 61 Revisited* (1965, Columbia Music; renewed 1993, Special Rider Music).

Chapter 2
Toby Keith, "No Honor Among Thieves," *Boomtown* (1994, Polygram Records).

Chapter 3
Dio, "Naked in the Rain," *Dream Evil* (1987, Ronnie James Dio).

Chapter 4
Eurythmics, "You Hurt Me & I Hate You," *We Too Are One* (RCA Records).
*It's just such application that perhaps also explains the more modern translation of this passage: "The words of a gossip are like choice morsels; they go down to a man's inmost parts" (Prov. 18:8, NIV).

Chapter 5
Red Hot Chili Peppers, "Under the Bridge," *Blood Sugar Sex Magik* (1992, Moebetoblame Music).

Chapter 6
Evanessence, "Bring Me to Life," *Fallen* (2003, Wind Up Entertain-ment, Inc.).

Chapter 7
Bono/U2, "When Love Comes to Town," *Rattle and Hum* (1988, Island Records, Inc.).

Chapter 8
Third Eye Blind, "I Want You," *Third Eye Blind* (1997) Electra Records/ EMI Music Publishing).

Chapter 9
David Wilcox, "In the Broken Places," *What You Whispered* (2000, David Wilcox, Midnight Ocean Bonfire Music & Soroka Music, Ltd.).

Chapter 10
Bjork, "All is Full of Love" (1997, Famous Music Corporation, Bjork Gudmundsdottir).

To order Pastor Bob Maddux's sermon series "Good Samaritan Therapy" in audio or video format, send an email to cla@clanet.com or write:

CLA Media Dept.
Christian Life Assembly
PO Box 307
Poway, California 92074

Visit the website of Christian Life Assembly where Bob Maddux is Senior Pastor at www.clanet.com.

Project Compassion is a medical mission co-founded by Bob Maddux providing medical care and the Good

News to people in over 22 nations over the past 11 years. Bob presently serves as an acting board member. Contact them at:

Project Compassion
11315 Rancho Bernardo Rd.
Suite 146
San Diego, CA 92127
www.project compassion.org

* Know + understand
  God's love.
* Be in God's presence-
  reflect on his love +
  glory.

"Run with it, run to
Jesus."

"You need to pure &
holy" - Pastor Ochoa.

* Listen to the truth-
truth brings healing.